MARIO LANZA

Derek Mannering was born in Dublin in 1948. He has lectured on film and television production in Ireland and recently directed a short film which was screened on RTE. He has also contributed to two radio programmes on Mario Lanza and his biography of the tenor has been written with the assistance both of Mario Lanza's family and friends in America. The author lives in Southern Ireland.

MARIO LANZA

A Biography

Derek Mannering

UNIVERSITY OF CALGARY PRESS
ROBERT HALE · LONDON

© Derek Mannering 1991
First published in Canada 1993
First published in Great Britain 1991
and paperback edition 1993

University of Calgary Press   Robert Hale Limited
2500 University Drive N.W.   Clerkenwell House
Calgary, Alberta, Canada T2N 1N4   Clerkenwell Green
                                     London EC1R 0HT

Canadian Cataloguing in Publication Data

Mannering, Derek, 1948–
  Mario Lanza : a biography

    Includes bibliographical references and index.
    ISBN 1-895176-35-2 (University of Calgary Press)—
    ISBN 0-7090-5052-6 (Robert Hale Limited)

    1. Lanza, Mario, 1921–1959.   2. Singers—
  United States—Biography.   I. Title.
  ML420.L36M36   1992   782.1'092   C92–091705–4

Printed in Great Britain by St. Edmundsbury Press.

Contents

For Jonathan
'The very best of everything in life always'

Illustrations

between pages 120 and 121

PICTURE CREDITS

British Mario Lanza Society: 1, 6, 11, 13, 17; Mario Lanza Institute, Philadelphia: 2, 3, 4; RCA, New York: 5; MGM–Corona: 7, 18; MGM: 8, 9; Associated Newspapers Ltd: 10; Terry Robinson: 12; Associated Press Ltd: 14; Daily Express: 15; United Press International (UK) Ltd: 16; P.A.–Reuter Features Ltd: 19.

Acknowledgements

Terry Robinson, the Lanza family, and the tenor's many friends in Philadelphia have all contributed, in one way or another, to the writing of this book and I am thankful also to Annamarie Callinicos for her warm reminiscences about her husband's time with Mario Lanza. Likewise, my thanks to Richard Mohr, Henri René and Peter Prichard for taking the time to share their memories of the man and his voice.

An entire chapter could be given over to the tireless efforts of the British Mario Lanza Society in providing me with so much information, and two people in particular – Pauline Franklin and Bill Earl – deserve major credit for ensuring the overall accuracy of the work. Their faith that I would pay fair and honest tribute to Mario Lanza was a commitment of trust in itself, and I hope they will consider the job to have been well and truthfully done.

I am especially grateful to Stephen Pattinson for his tremendous support and enthusiasm in researching the Discography, and thanks are due also to Daniel Guss and Bernard Lozea of BMG Classics in New York, and Paolo Rossi of BMG in Rome, for their help in completing the exercise.

The task of sourcing the many interviews used throughout the book could not have been done without the generous co-operation of Clyde Smith in America and John Rice in Ireland, and for all the articles, photographs etc. supplied to me by Lanza admirers the world over, my thanks to Vincent de Fini, Tony Partington, Joseph Curreri, Barbara Knight, Patricia Smith, Paul Velda, Dora Alker, Richard Stevenson, Tom Balfe, Phyllis Savage,

Christy and Marie Smith, and James O'Connor – and my apologies to anyone I have inadvertently left out.

It is a great privilege for me to have José Carreras lend his very distinguished name to my work, and I am extremely grateful to Penelope Marland of the John Coast Agency in London, for acting on my behalf in this regard. Thanks also to Frank Powis, who generously allowed me access to John Coast's personal file on Mario Lanza, to Margaret Litabarski, of the José Carreras Society, and to Elaine, for her help and advice and to Vincent Boyle, who first introduced me to the glorious voice of Mario Lanza so many years ago.

Finally, to Kate, the most important thank you of all. Her unequivocal support, encouragement and belief in me throughout the writing of this book ensured, in the end, that the story of Mario Lanza here told, is a complete and true one.

Derek Mannering, 1991

Foreword

I was a small boy of seven, growing up in Barcelona, when I first discovered Mario Lanza through his remarkable film *The Great Caruso*. That wonderful voice and the charismatic appeal of his personality had a profound effect on my life and I decided there and then that I too would one day sing the great operatic roles so persuasively portrayed on screen by the young American tenor.

Mario Lanza influenced a whole generation of singers through that one film. His dramatic, expansive singing style and larger-than-life temperament helped make him the most talked about tenor since Caruso, an artist with whom he was closely associated throughout his career. Like Caruso before him, he was able to interest even the most casual listener in the delights and joys of grand opera and his recording of arias from the Caruso film became the first operatic collection in history to sell over one million copies. To achieve all of that by the age of thirty, with only two stage performances of *Madama Butterfly* to his credit, was an astonishing feat in itself and a pointed reminder to his critics who felt he was short changing a God-given talent.

It is a sad fact though, that Mario Lanza did not devote more time to the classical stage – what triumphs he would have enjoyed! But then time was already running out even as *The Great Caruso* was breaking box office records throughout the world. Tragically, the world lost a unique artist when Mario Lanza died in Rome at the absurdly young age of thirty-eight. Yet his talent, like that of Caruso, lives on through the medium of recorded sound. To hear again that glorious, ringing tenor, that freshness and vitality of performance that was his and his alone, is to be reminded once more of Lanza's very special place in the annals of twentieth-century popular music.

As Derek Mannering points out in his exhaustive study of a fascinating career, Mario Lanza was a true original. To millions of people the world over, myself included, his magnificent voice enriched our lives and introduced us to a wider spectrum of classical and popular music through his films and recordings. That in itself, is surely a wonderful legacy for any artist to be remembered by.

José Carreras

Introduction

In a darkened cinema, the young boy sits enthralled. Up there, on the screen, his idol sings like a god. Big man, bigger voice. Never mind that the approach to the music is at times a little overstated, the singing less refined than it should be; this is Hollywood, after all, playing at being Italian. No, what really matters is the spirit of the thing: the soul of the great musical masters being invoked up there by that impossibly assured and handsome American. The man they are calling the new Caruso ...

Even back in the early 1950s, the young José Carreras knew that the man on the screen was no secondhand Caruso, or Gigli, or anybody else for that matter. This man, this young American movie star, was something else entirely. Unique and unclassifiable in his own special way, he was blessed with the sort of once-in-a-lifetime voice that made even the most tired and jaded music sound fresh and new. He was a super star, long before that much-abused word was ever coined, and a man whose highly charged talents went on to influence a whole generation of other great artists.

To Luciano Pavarotti, he is simply 'my idol'; a vivid reminder of a time when youthful ideals and aspirations were soon to become reality. Carreras freely acknowledges his own debt to the man by citing *The Great Caruso* as the single most important factor in his decision to become an opera star. And Placido Domingo helped legitimize his memory, and his reputation, by hosting a television tribute, *An American Caruso*, in his name.

In his time, Mario Lanza was arguably the most famous singer of grand opera in the world, yet he was not an 'opera' star in the strictest sense of the word. In a professional career that spanned little more than a decade, he never once found time to record a complete operatic performance, and his on-stage appearances in that particular medium were limited to a mere two. Yet, in the short term, he did more to popularize good music, and opera in particular, than scores of his more readily acclaimed and legitimate contemporaries, becoming, in the course of a turbulent and all too brief career, the most genuinely popular tenor since Caruso.

In his private, as well as his public life, he lived much as he sang – with drama, passion and more than a little notoriety. Volatile and temperamental, charming and self-effacing; he was a combination of all things to all people, yet there were few who would say that they knew him well. To those who did call him friend, the loyalty was never in doubt. Each year, in his home town of Philadelphia, friends and admirers alike gather to pay tribute and remember. Musical scholarships are awarded in his name, always in the hope that somehow, someday, a worthy successor to his own remarkable talent will be found.

But it is unlikely that we will ever find another Mario Lanza. That unique vitality of performance, that romantic panache which seemed to infuse practically everything he touched, was his and his alone. The American success story supreme, with more than a little tragedy thrown in for good measure.

An American Caruso? How about Mario Lanza, Tenor? That would be more than enough to describe the man and his talent, and its simplicity would have pleased him.

D.M.

1 Tenor

When Arturo Toscanini first heard Mario Lanza sing in the mid-1940s, his praise for the tenor's natural talent was unstinting. It was, he maintained, 'the greatest voice of the twentieth century'.

Given the conductor's close association with Enrico Caruso several decades earlier, it was probably the single greatest compliment ever paid to the young American tenor. It was also, conversely, the most misunderstood, for Toscanini never intended to imply that Mario Lanza was a better singer than his illustrious predecessor. Caruso's achievements had come only after years of spartan self-discipline and study, an almost obsessive pursuit of vocal perfection which, coupled with an endless, gruelling round of appearances on every major concert and operatic platform throughout the world, undoubtedly helped contribute to his untimely passing at the age of forty-eight. By the end of that life, Caruso had come to personify the very highest standard of excellence in bold, colourful and imaginative singing. The 'tenor's tenor', his innate artistry became a focal point of reference for every classical male vocalist since. He was certainly the yardstick by which the young Mario Lanza set his own career goals back in the 1940s, and Toscanini's remarkable commendation, coming at a time when the American tenor was searching for his own particular niche in musical history, must have set his heart, if not his ambition, spinning.

What Toscanini was complimenting in the Lanza voice was, of course, the natural beauty of its timbre: a 'wall' of pure, God-given sound which, in the right hands and with the right encouragement, might well surpass the accomplishments of even the great Caruso himself. The early Caruso voice had been more baritone than tenor, the famous 'high C' being achieved only through diligent practice and more than a little determination. Lanza, on the other hand, had no such problems. From the very moment the boy discovered he had 'a voice', its sheer range and power was, and would remain, a source of constant amazement to all who heard it. Indeed, it has often been said that if Lanza had had to work a little harder to achieve what was his to command, the resulting tragedies of his life might well have been averted entirely. In a sense, it was just too easy for him, and to Toscanini and many of his contemporaries at that time, there was never any doubt that a glorious future awaited the man who was even then being hailed as the American Caruso. That the golden future was triumphantly achieved there can be no doubt, but Mario Lanza's decision to pursue that career in a somewhat different direction – 'the path not taken', as Domingo put it – undoubtedly resulted in one of the most deeply felt losses to classical music that this century has seen. Peter Herman Adler, musical director of NBC Opera and the man responsible for conducting the operatic excerpts featured in Lanza's film *The Great Caruso*, saw the tragedy for what it was: 'Opera singers are like wild animals. They must be trained, kept in strict discipline. Ten years with the right opera company and no one could compare with him. But after being a star, how could he go back to training?'[1]

Lanza's association with Caruso, which persisted throughout his entire career, began literally with the date of his birth – 31 January 1921, the year which ironically marked the passing of the great Italian tenor in Naples. The only child of Antonio and Maria Lanza Cocozza, from whom he would later take his professional name, Alfred Arnold Cocozza first saw the light of day in a tiny, cramped first-floor bedroom above his grandfather's grocery shop at 636 Christian Street, in an area of south Philadelphia which was then known as 'Little Italy'. Both of 'Freddy's' parents were born in Italy. Antonio Cocozza had emigrated to America at the age of sixteen from his home town of Filignano. Ironically, one of his first jobs in the New World was varnishing cabinets for RCA Records, the company which had recorded the great Caruso and would later reap vast fortunes from its exclusive contract with Tony's son. With the outbreak of war, Antonio Cocozza joined the 37th 145th Infantry, and it was during the battle of the Meuse-Argonne forest, soon after capturing a German prisoner, that he was seriously wounded by one of the notorious 'dum dums', or split-head bullets. The bullet completely shattered the lower part of his right arm, an injury which brought him back to civilian life with a total disability pension and an uncertain future. A chance encounter in south Philadelphia soon after, however, completely changed his life, for it was here that he met the sixteen-year-old girl who, in the short space of six weeks, would become his wife. Maria Lanza had arrived in America from Abruzzi when she was just six months old. Her father, Salvatore, was a businessman to the manner born, initially finding work selling vegetables from a horse and cart along the Philadelphia Main Line. A more permanent outlet was eventually established at a property located at 636 Christian Street; it was a small, two-storey building which somehow managed to house Salvatore, his wife and their eight children, along with the grocery store which provided the family with its income. By the time she was of age, Maria took turns with her brothers and sisters in helping out with the daily running of the store and it was here, on a sunny afternoon in 1919, that Antonio Cocozza walked into her life. Tony had wandered in for the less than romantic reason of purchasing salami, but to Maria, who saw only a handsome, 26-year-old veteran resplendent in army uniform, it was the classic scenario of love at first sight. Following a simple ceremony a few weeks later, the newly-weds moved into the already overcrowded conditions at Christian Street. Their joy was complete when Maria gave birth to her only son, Alfred Arnold – or 'Freddy', as they always called him – born at 9.45 a.m. on the last day of January and idolized to distraction by both parents throughout his life.

The baby was baptized at the nearby church of St Mary Magdalene di Pazzi, which has the distinction of being Philadelphia's first Catholic Church and where, another irony, the celebrant was a certain Father Caruso. The cornerstone of both families' heritage was an impressive collection of mostly worn 78 rpm records by some of the great voices of the day. Caruso, Ruffo, Pertile – the house was filled with their singing and it was this vibrant legacy that provided the earliest musical grounding for the future Mario Lanza. Much to everyone's delight, the boy took an almost instant liking to this rich and predominantly Italian art form, and it is a well-recorded fact that at the age of seven, Freddy Cocozza once listened to Caruso's famous recording of Pagliacci's lament over twenty-five times at a single sitting.

When the boy was nine, the Cocozzas left Salvatore Lanza to his store and moved to 2040 Mercy Street, a two-storey, red-brick house with six small rooms and a bath, which was a vast improvement on the cramped conditions at Christian Street. The boy grew up, attending St Mary Magdalene di Pazzi School on 7th and Montrose. Nare Junior High School and Southern High School followed, where his teachers discovered that Freddy Cocozza would rather play baseball than study. He became a rebellious, reluctant pupil and it was soon clear that discipline, or rather the lack of it, was destined to be the one major stumbling block in Alfred Cocozza's life. Put simply, Freddy Cocozza hated conformity in whatever guise it took; a definite character flaw which would have even greater repercussions in the professional years still to come. The first real indication that the boy had a singing voice came on a summer's day in 1937, when he was sixteen years old. Popular legend has it that he was listening yet again to a recording of Caruso, 'Vesti la giubba', when he began to sing along with it, this time in a voice of great natural power and tonal quality. Certainly, the fullness of the voice was overwhelming; a voice, moreover, which only gained in richness and quality as the years went by.

His first audition took place before a local baritone,

Antonio Scarduzzo, who wisely cautioned the young man against the dangers of pushing the voice too much too soon. Scarduzzo felt that the singing lessons proper should wait a year or two, with greater effort in the meantime directed towards language studies and an instrument, possibly piano. Then, when the voice had settled, vocal exercises could begin in earnest. Scarduzzo also directed the boy to the study of solfeggio and the sight-reading of music but this, surprisingly, proved to be the one particular area of music which Mario Lanza could never quite master. Constantine Callinicos, his principal conductor and accompanist in later years, speculated on the reasons behind this peculiar shortcoming:

> He had a kind of aversion regarding the theoretical side of music and mostly learning solfeggio, which is not such a difficult thing. But somehow he must have fallen into the hands of somebody who drove him to hate solfeggio, which he knew would help him in learning scores, in every facet of his work.[2]

Solfeggio notwithstanding, the boy did study intently for over eighteen months, although Scarduzzo's advice to limit the singing was not always taken seriously.

> His grandfather had a home in Wildwood, New Jersey, and Freddy got a summer job there, driving a trolley car. We used to wait at a certain corner and we could hear when his car was coming five blocks away, because we could hear him singing ... 'O sole mio' or something ... and lo and behold, we'd all get on the trolley car for nothing, like he owned the transportation company.[3]

By now the entire family was convinced that a professional career was definitely on the cards for the boy, and in the many discussions which took place at home about that future, the suitability – or otherwise – of his remaining 'Alfred Cocozza' frequently came up. It was generally felt that something more dramatic, more romantic, was necessary if the boy was to become a success. In the 1983 television documentary, *Mario Lanza – An American Caruso*, tenor Placido Domingo visits the

family home on Christian Street and displays a school copy
book from that early period. There, in the boy's own hand,
is a list of potential names: 'Al Lanza', 'Al Cocozza', 'Fred
Lanza' ... until finally, in the very last column on the very
last page ... 'Mario Lanza'. It was an appropriate choice,
'Lanza', in particular, conjuring up an image of Mediter-
ranean passion so in keeping with his expansive style of
singing. The name change neatly coincided with his first
real period of professional voice training, under the guidance of soprano Irene Williams, a former opera star of some
distinction, with whom he would spend the next eighteen
months. For the young Mario Lanza, all the months of
frustration were cast aside, as he proceeded to let forth with
the most glorious, natural-sounding notes Miss Williams
had ever heard from a pupil. Lanza's top notes were
dazzling, but what pleased the teacher almost as much was
the assured and confident lower register – that 'fullness' of
sound which, as time went by, would recall the latter-day
Caruso voice, if not the great man's style of singing.

By now too, stories about the 'golden voice' were
circulating throughout the city and from time to time, Miss
Williams took the opportunity of presenting her pupil in
recital at a number of Philadelphia's most elite society
homes. Earl Denny, a popular bandleader in Philadelphia
at that time, invited him to sing the Bach-Gounod 'Ave
Maria' at St Mary Magdalene di Pazzi Church on
Christmas morning, 1940, and the tenor's intense and
deeply felt performance is reported to have moved many
parishioners to tears. It was that sort of voice, and Irene
Williams, for one, knew that the time was fast
approaching for Lanza to move on to a more advanced
regimen of studies than she could provide. The problem,
as always, was money – or the lack of it – and clearly some
form of sponsorship had to be found. The answer came
through a man named William K. Huff, concert manager
at the Philadelphia Academy of Music, who had heard
Lanza sing at one of Miss Williams's society recitals and
who was aware of his current plight.

Conductor Serge Koussevitsky was due to give a
concert at the Academy and Huff felt that if the maestro

heard Lanza sing, something might be done to help further his career. Something was, the direct result of an impromptu audition about which, initially, Koussevitsky knew nothing.

> The concert was over and we got into one of the dressing rooms opposite the one Koussevitsky was using ... and Mr Huff told me 'Now you start to sing.' There was a piano in each of the dressing rooms, so I started to sing what I call my 'lucky' aria, 'Vesti la giubba' ... Just when I finished, Koussevitsky put both arms around me, kissed me in true Russian style and said 'You will come and live with me in the Berkshires.'
>
> I realized at that moment that something terrific was happening in my life, in my career ... and this was the beginning of the most glorious period of my life.[4]

It would also prove to be the most intensive period of training and study that Mario Lanza would undertake for several years to come. A delighted Irene Williams even took the trouble to see off her former pupil at the train station, with a stern warning to concentrate on the studies and stay away from girls. Sensing too, that the voice was now surely destined for great things, she also had him sign a contract guaranteeing her 5 per cent of any singing income he received over $5,000 a year, and 10 per cent if that sum exceeded $7,500; a safeguard, she maintained, aimed at protecting her protégé from unscrupulous talent agents who might defraud him. For his part, Lanza would probably have signed away his entire career, so great was his 'mental and emotional excitement' at that time. His outgoing nature, by and large, led him to trust everyone with whom he came into contact and, like a great many other impulsive gestures he would make in the years to come, the 'contract' with Irene Williams was something he would come to regret.

The list of graduates over the years from the Berkshire School of Music at Tanglewood, Massachusetts, reads like a 'who's who' of great modern composers, singers and conductors. It was Koussevitsky's dream to provide the finest training programme for talented musicians under the guidance of some of the best teachers in the land, and the quiet, idyllic surroundings proved a perfect launching pad for the young tenor. Among his fellow students that summer were conductor Lukas Foss, and Koussevitsky's new protégé and assistant, an exciting young composer, conductor and pianist by the name of Leonard Bernstein. Lanza was coached for a time by Bernstein but he was not, by most accounts, a particularly diligent pupil. What he wanted to do, simply and basically, was to sing. His natural voice production was spectacularly good, and he felt little need to subject it to the sort of intensive training and demanding vocal studies set down by the school. But his time at Tanglewood undoubtedly did pay dividends. By the time his scholarship had come to an end, in August 1942, Lanza had gained immeasurably in vocal confidence and style. He was heard to excellent effect in his coming-out performance as Fenton, in Otto Nicolai's comic opera, *The Merry Wives of Windsor*, on the night of 7 August 1942. Lanza had previously sung Rodolfo in a workshop production of *La Bohème*, but this once-off performance marked the first time he had sung a complete role before the general public. Under the direction of Herbert Graf, the opera department at Tanglewood staged an impressive production in English of the seldom heard work, and it was soon clear from a subsequent review in the *New York Times* by eminent critic, Noel Straus, just who among the large cast had garnered the lion's share of praise.

> Another outstanding member of the cast was a young tenor, Mario Lanza, in the part of Fenton. If Lanza's natural abilities are developed in the proper direction, he will own a splendid voice. At present he needs more fundamental training and rudiments of style. Yet even now, he offers good musicality and diction.[5]

Even at that early stage of his career, Lanza posed a striking figure. Resplendent in period costume, plumed hat tilted rakishly to one side, the very image hinted at 'star quality'. Ironically though, the one remaining photograph from that production at Tanglewood was to prove curiously prophetic. With the entire cast gathered together for a curtain call, Lanza is seen standing alone, stage right, away from the company; isolated even then from a world of which he would never fully be part.

Following the performance, Lanza returned to Philadelphia where among the many letters and telegrams of congratulation awaiting him was one from the President of the United States, instructing Alfred Arnold Cocozza to report for duty in the US Army.

The year was 1942, and with the world at war, the projected career launch of the American Caruso was temporarily put on hold.

2   The American Caruso

With the possible exception of the two years in Hollywood which followed the *Student Prince* fiasco in 1952, Lanza's army stint was easily the unhappiest period of his young life. It is not hard to see why. For one thing, the newly christened Mario Lanza suddenly found himself plain Alfred Cocozza again; Private Cocozza no. 423 AAF BU to be exact, stationed in the very hot and very dusty Forces base in Marfa, Texas. Then there was the question of discipline; this had been a very definite problem in Philadelphia and was now a very definite requisite for the situation in which he found himself. Subjected to all sorts of gruelling physical exercises and duty rosters, Lanza quickly despaired, turning, as he would always do in times of stress, to food. In the space of a few short months, the tenor came to weigh almost 260 lb, his heaviest ever, and a far cry from the relatively slim young singer who had thrilled audiences at Tanglewood.

But any possibility that Private Cocozza might be considered for overseas duty was soon abandoned when the army discovered just who it was they had in their midst: the 'army', that is, in the guise of Corporal Johnny Silver, a diminutive, 5ft 2in ex-burlesque comic whose job it was to put together variety acts which toured the numerous bases throughout the country. Not surprisingly, Silver was overwhelmed when he first heard the mighty voice and, like William Huff before him, determined to do all he could to help further Lanza's career, army duties notwithstanding. The opportunity presented itself sooner than expected with the arrival at Marfa of impresario Peter Lind Hayes, an air force sergeant who had written a musical with Frank Loesser called *On the Beam*. Hayes was touring the bases looking for talent and Silver lost no time in telling him about the 'Forces' Caruso'. An audition was arranged for the following day and what happened next varies with each telling. The most popular story, and one which Lanza himself often enjoyed recounting, was that of a gifted tenor, his throat inflamed by the red dust of the army base, who found himself unable to sing at the scheduled audition. Enter the resourceful Corporal Silver, who has the ingenious idea of pasting a label with Lanza's name over a recording of Metropolitan opera star Frederick Jagel singing an aria from *Tosca*, and presents it to Hayes as a 'stand-in' until the tenor is well enough to perform. Then, when the inevitable day arrives, Hayes will be heard to proclaim 'You sound even better in person.'

Larry Adler's brother Jerry, a gifted harmonica player in his own right, was part of the troupe and recalls a slightly different – and less romantic – scenario: The whole story is completely untrue regarding the dry panhandle dust. Mario never did have a sore throat in Marfa and I was present when he sang his beautiful heart out in the base theatre for us. The entire story is pure nonsense, although it looks awfully good in print.[1]

Whatever the truth, Lanza got the job and sang out the remainder of the war in a steady stream of concerts throughout army bases across America, where he was invariably tagged the 'Forces' Caruso'. It was hardly the sort of 'fundamental training' that Noel Straus had encouraged at Tanglewood, but it did at least give him the opportunity to exercise his vocal cords and develop more stage presence. His final engagement with the army came with the show *Winged Victory*, a flag waving, play-cum-musical put together by noted producer and playwright Moss Hart. The production showcased the talents of actors Gary Merrill, Karl Malden and Edmond O'Brien among its huge cast of servicemen, and following a try-out at Boston's Schubert Theatre, opened at the 44th Street Playhouse in New York in November 1943. For the successful duration of the show's run, which carried over to May of the following year, the combined efforts of the cast and production crew managed to produce a weekly return of over $25,000 which went directly to the Army Emergency Relief Fund. When the film options of *Winged Victory* were taken up by 20th Century Fox, the entire cast moved to Hollywood, where the show was transferred to the screen by director George Cukor.

Strictly speaking, this was Mario Lanza's first screen appearance, although 'appearance' is perhaps not the most appropriate word, given that the tenor's talents were relegated to a fifty-man choral group under the direction of Lt. Leonard de Paur. Moss Hart later claimed that he had no idea that a voice of such magnitude was hidden in the chorus, but *Winged Victory*, such as it was, was hardly the type of show to highlight an up-and-coming opera star. But the voice was being noticed. Lanza's friendship with actors such as Barry Nelson and Walter Pidgeon led to an ever-increasing round of parties at many of the top Hollywood homes where, naturally, he was expected to sing for his supper. Lanza was only too happy to oblige, thrilled at being in the presence of people he had previously seen only on the silver screen. Frank Sinatra was a big fan and did what he could to spread the good word: 'The kid knocked a hole through me. Talk about people swooning when I sing, the tables were turned when I heard Lanza. I immediately asked him if he wanted to be on my programme but he was not able to accept any contracts. He happens to be in the army.'[2]

Everyone, it seemed, loved the voice, but no one – least of all Lanza – considered it suitable for anything other than the opera stage. Apart from the occasional popular solo from the likes of Deanna Durbin or Allan Jones, grand opera had never made the successful transition to motion pictures. Even Caruso's two starring roles were in silent films. Then too, there was the vexing question of Mario Lanza's appearance, for while there was no denying his good looks and easy charm, those three unhappy years in the army had played havoc with his waistline. A potential leading man he most certainly was not. But the Hollywood exposure was helping, for it was at one of these parties, at the home of actress Irene Manning, that he met Art Rush, a top Hollywood agent who was deeply impressed by the voice. With Rush's help, Lanza signed a $3,000 student contract with RCA Records; this generous allowance enabled him to continue with his studies until he was ready to record for the company. It was the first time in RCA's 44-year history that a virtual unknown had been signed to their prestigious Red Seal Classical label. Capturing Lanza had been the final coup in a year which saw the record company add Leonard Bernstein, baritone Robert Merrill and mezzo-soprano Blanche Thebom to its ever-increasing list of outstanding artists. Miss Thebom would eventually join Lanza on the MGM soundstages in Hollywood when it came time to film *The Great Caruso* in 1951, but both stars were very much in their ascendancy in the mid-1940s.

Lanza's eventual release from the army came on 29 January 1945, when he received a medical discharge from McCaw General Hospital in Walla Walla, Washington, on the grounds of having incurred 'defective hearing' during his time in service. If it seemed a curious reason for discharge, Lanza didn't wait to argue and returned immediately to New York in the company of a friend, Bert Hicks. Hicks, who came from Chicago, had a sister, Betty, living in New York – an attractive, dark-haired girl who was soon to become Mrs Mario Lanza. Despite their different ethnic backgrounds – she was part Irish – Mario and Betty Lanza's marriage was a close one; it was blessed with four children in its fourteen-year span and survived what at times must have seemed like well-nigh insurmountable odds during the tenor's volatile career. They were married before Judge Griffin at Beverly Hills City Hall on 13 April 1945, in a civil ceremony which came as a great shock to Lanza's over-protective and Catholic mother when the newly-weds arrived in Philadelphia and announced it the following day. Given the circumstances of her son's marriage – and an only son at that – it was hardly surprising that Maria Cocozza should view her new daughter-in-law with more than a little suspicion, and in truth, the two women would never be completely comfortable in each other's company.

Minor conflict notwithstanding, the Lanzas returned to New York soon after, with a promise to arrange a church ceremony as quickly as possible. This eventually took place in July, in the tiny Manhattan church of St Columbo, and was attended by both families and a few close friends. The Lanzas' living accommodation was taken care of by their new friend Robert Weede, a gifted baritone from the Metropolitan Opera Company, whom Lanza had met through his contacts with Art Rush. When Weede heard of the newly-weds' plight – little money and a one-room apartment – he generously offered them the use of his own place free of charge. Weede preferred to commute from his home in Nyack, just outside New York, and the Lanzas took the opportunity to move into his exclusive, four-room, fourth-floor apartment overlooking the Rockefeller Center. The Lanza luck was starting to turn and it was also through Weede that Mario received his first real break as a professional singer, when he was surprisingly chosen to stand in for tenor Jan Peerce as an occasional replacement on ABC radio's popular *Celanese* show.

Weede was a regular guest on the weekly programme, entitled *Great Moments in Music*, and Lanza had attended many of the broadcasts, clearly delighted to be in the presence of an artist of Peerce's stature. Indeed, when it came to vocal refinement and phrasing, Lanza was not in the same class as Peerce, but he had that special 'something' in his voice which prompted the producers – encouraged in no small way by Weede – to give him a chance. It was a faith more than justified by the young tenor's subsequent performances. Between 24 October 1945 and 20 February 1946, Lanza appeared in a total of six programmes, the format of which – operatic excerpts one week, popular songs the next – curiously anticipated his own eventual repertoire and style of singing. While existing tapes of these programmes show him to be slightly stiff, or cold in performance – he is even heard to forget the words to 'America the Beautiful' on one of the shows – his overall approach to the music is singularly impressive. The relative ease with which he moved from Verdi one week to Irving Berlin the next, was remarkable in one so young and inexperienced, particularly when one considers that the shows were broadcast live.

Despite the valuable exposure though, Lanza himself was not entirely pleased with the series: 'It wasn't a happy experience. I was required to sing things which were so difficult ... I needed years of experience before tackling them ... Verdi's *Otello*, for instance. After six programmes, I knew I couldn't go on.'[3]

Lanza was now studying under Polly Robinson, a voice coach who had rehearsal rooms at the prestigious Carnegie Hall in Manhattan. It was through her that he was introduced to another pupil, Sam Weiler, a chance encounter which had a profound effect on both their lives.

Weiler was a successful businessman who, with his brother Jack, operated the Fairmont and St Francis hotels in San Francisco. What he wanted most however, was to sing, and his light if unexceptional voice was regularly put through its paces by Miss Robinson's careful tutoring. Weiler's passion for opera was almost as great as Lanza's, so when the two met by chance one day in the Carnegie building, Polly Robinson persuaded her star pupil to sing an aria for the businessman. Weiler sat and listened – and the lives of both men were changed forever: 'I knew there and then that I had just heard the greatest voice in the world.'[4]

It would be wrong to say that Weiler was intimidated by the Lanza voice. It went much deeper than that. He knew, quite simply, that his own career as a singer had no future – certainly when compared to a voice of Lanza's calibre – but he felt that he still could be a party, through that voice, to a career of unequalled magnitude. After the lesson was over, the two men lingered for hours in a nearby coffee shop where, for the most part, Mario Lanza talked and Sam Weiler listened. At the end of it all, Lanza had not only found a business manager but a generous benefactor into the bargain. For 10 per cent of the singer's future earnings, Weiler agreed to take care of all his current debts, which by now ran to several thousand dollars, pay him a weekly stipend to live on, and cover all expenses incurred in his singing lessons, whatever they might be. It was an extraordinary gesture on Weiler's part and it was little wonder that he was eventually asked to be godfather to the Lanzas' first child a few years later.

Aside from his genuine fondness for Mario Lanza, Weiler was an astute businessman, and for him to make such a huge financial commitment to a relative unknown spoke volumes for the outstanding quality of the tenor's voice at that time. Weiler decided too, that in terms of vocal training, only the very best would do, and it was through his many contacts in the New York music circle that he eventually arranged for Lanza to audition for Enrico Rosati, famed voice coach to the great Beniamino Gigli. Rosati's reaction to the Lanza voice was typical: 'I have waited thirty-four years for you [since Gigli]. You have a voice blessed by God.'[5] In truth, Lanza did require the quality of coaching that only someone like Rosati could provide, and so, with Weiler easing the strain of his financial worries, the stage was set for the transformation of a rough-cut vocal diamond into a true gem.

In all, Lanza spent fifteen months with Rosati, and if at times the path was strewn with frustration and doubt – the problem of discipline again – Rosati persisted as best he could, instilling not only craftsmanship and finesse into Lanza's performance but also, and just as importantly, confidence. Lanza never forgot his time with Rosati and when he departed in 1946, he left behind a signed photograph with the heartfelt inscription:

> To Maestro Enrico Rosati – any success I am having or will have in the future I owe 100 per cent to you, the greatest undisputed voice teacher in the world, past, present and future. I love you, and you will always be close to me wherever I am or in whatever I do. Especially on stage, you will always be there in the third register. All my love for you, Maestro. Mario Lanza.[6]

A few years later, when he had made his first real impression in Hollywood, Lanza recalled his work with the great teacher:

It was both rich and difficult. Slowly and painstakingly he built my voice into what it is today, so that I am able to sing for hours without tiring. Also, under Rosati, I had to practise every day to achieve what the Italians call Bel Canto. Eventually, Rosati and Edward Johnson of Metropolitan Opera in New York invited me to join the company, but without the necessary time to prepare for it in peace, I did not think it would be an advisable step to take. I didn't want to be placed in front of the world's largest opera audience without first completing an extensive study of the operatic works and until I had reached a reasonable standard of artistic representation and maturity.[7]

That Lanza was able to turn his back on such an offer indicates one of two things: either he was still insecure and plagued with self-doubts about his vocal abilities or, conversely, he had such confidence in the voice and where it would take him, that even the Metropolitan could wait. In a sense, it was a little of both. He knew that despite Rosati's coaching, his voice was still not fully polished or developed. But that meant even more rigorous training, more years of labouring over solfeggio and all those difficult exercises he had grown to hate. And even then, his admittance to the Metropolitan would, of necessity, be very much a low-key affair. No grand entrance for the man now being hailed as the logical successor to the great Caruso. Weiler by now had signed him under contract to the prestigious Columbia Artists' Management, a move which both men felt would considerably enhance the tenor's earning potential. So, for the time being, the concert platform won; in fairness to Lanza, though he was also anxious to start showing some return to his benefactor for what by now had become a considerable financial investment: 'Mr Weiler worried about paying for my instruction and my travel expenses. He also provided me with my clothes and all my other necessities. He must have handled $60,000 for me.'[8]

Arthur Judson, head of Columbia Artists, saw to it that the tenor embarked on a well-chosen series of recitals and concerts throughout the United States and Canada. On 10

October 1945, Lanza joined soprano Agnes Davis and accompanist Josef Blatt for a concert at Montcalm Palace, in Quebec, the local newspaper erroneously listing them as 'artists from the Metropolitan Opera'. Not that it really mattered. Those who heard Mario Lanza sing at that time would have believed him worthy of any opera stage in the world. The review of the Quebec concert, with its incisive and peculiarly prophetic closing comment, was typical of the sort of response which greeted him wherever he went:

> Mr Lanza, though still very young, has a rich and expressive voice and does not seem to be afraid of the difficulties. The variety of his art, his interpretation possibilities, his magnificent voice, invited us to admire this exceptionally gifted tenor. He is able to interest even those who do not like classical music.[9]

By the time he had reached Ontario, for a concert in November 1946, he was virtually a sensation.

> Just a few lines to let you know what a tremendous impression Mr Lanza made on our audience last night. It was impossible for him to leave. He was even forced to repeat one of his encores. From both an artist's and a personal point of view I don't think it will ever be possible for me to get such a thrill from presenting any artist. The privilege of having Mr Lanza with us is definitely the high point of my career as a promoter. I doubt if it will ever be equalled. Dr de Ridder, our conducter, said that in his experience he has never had a soloist who was so wonderful to work with. I know that this 'local manager to New York office' letter has got to be more or less routine in this business. But for once please don't chalk this up as the same old baloney. This is the real thing and we hope we'll have the thrill of presenting Mr Lanza, many, many times down through the years.[10]

Five months later, on 14 April 1947, Lanza was booked for a recital at the State Teachers' College Auditorium, in Shippensburg, Pennsylvania, and it was at this unlikely venue that he first met the man who, more than any other, would remain closest to him musically throughout the remainder of his career. Constantine Callinicos was a New York born musician of Greek extraction who, like Lanza, was just starting out on his chosen career. A graduate of Manhattan's Julliard School of Music and sometime composer, Callinicos – or 'Costa', as Lanza affectionately came to call him – had already developed a reputation as a skilled accompanist when he was approached by Columbia Artists for what was to be a one-off engagement at Shippensburg.

Callinicos freely admitted that he had never even heard of the town, let alone the tenor, but finding himself between bookings at the time, agreed to do the recital. His first conversation with Mario Lanza however, did not augur well for a successful engagement, for having telephoned the tenor to set a date for rehearsal, Lanza promptly cried off: 'We don't need to rehearse. I've got things to do. I have confidence in you, Constantine ...'

Lanza's ability to dumbfound and astonish his audience, usually through his singing, here took on an entirely different slant. Anticipating a disaster of major proportions. Callinicos almost backed out there and then, but something about the voice at the other end of the telephone – an exuberant warmth and almost boyish enthusiasm – held him in check. The two finally met at the train station in the tiny Pennsylvania town on 14 April, just two hours before the concert was due to begin.

> He was just twenty-six with a simple, ingenuous vigour that I had rarely seen among professional artists. He had the build and barrel chest of a heavyweight fighter and was in excellent shape. Betty was a lively brunette of medium height with a trim figure ... as wholesome as the girl next door.[11]

Betty Lanza had by now made it her usual practice to accompany her husband on tour whenever possible, and while she would never share Mario Lanza's passion for classical music, her support and admiration for his talent was never found wanting. They undoubtedly made a charming couple and Callinicos was impressed by what he saw. But he had still to hear Mario Lanza sing, and his

sense of unease quickly returned when the tenor
announced that he had forgotten his tuxedo, requesting
instead that they both appear in business suits. Lanza's
loathing of formality was surfacing yet again, and the
'forgotten tuxedo' excuse would reappear many times
over in the concert years that lay ahead. So it was then,
that the two men, wearing lounge suits, stepped on to the
stage at the State Teachers' Auditorium to face an
audience of over 5,000 people, most of whom – like
Callinicos – had no idea of the surprise that lay in store.

> As I started the introduction to 'Pieta Signore' by Stradella,
> a favourite of Enrico Caruso's, Mario turned his back on
> the audience. Leaning casually over the piano, he winked,
> then smiled at me. Then he began singing, and I knew that
> the tux was unimportant and that the offensive,
> tradition-defying back-to-the-audience was just a neo-
> phyte's lack of stage deportment. For as the rich, glorious
> tones flowed effortlessly through Mario's throat, I knew I
> was listening to one of the greatest tenor voices since
> Caruso. Through Mario's vocal cords, and through those
> bony cavities in his throat, nose and mouth which are
> called the resonators, emerged phrases of such opulence,
> warmth and velvety quality that I sat there feeling some
> incredible joke had been played on me. The notes were
> round and lush, satisfying and meaningful, and his breath
> control, on the long phrases, was truly amazing.[12]

Although neither artist realized it at the time, a bond
was formed that night in Shippensburg that would
develop and grow through all the fantastic successes – and
more than a few tribulations – that were soon to come into
the life of Mario Lanza. Callinicos never doubted for one
instant that Lanza was set to become one of the most
outstanding tenors of his generation: not so much an
American Caruso as, simply, Mario Lanza, unique and
blessed with his own highly individual talent and style.
From their very first recording session together in New
York, in 1949, through the fabulous film and concert-hall
successes that would follow, 'Costa's' contribution to the
tenor's career was well-nigh inestimable. He was always
there. Always encouraging, always trying to guide Lanza

down the musical path his talent, if not his ambition, seemed to dictate.

In time, as Mario Lanza came more and more to depend on Callinicos's support and understanding, the conductor came to realize that his own particular niche in a unique part of musical history was linked inexorably to his friend. And it was more than just allegiance to a magnificent voice:

> Mario was like a brother to me. And it wasn't because he was generous to offer RCA Victor guarantees in order for me to start recording with him. It was that natural empathy and sympathy that I had with the man. He had such a big heart that you couldn't help but love him. Really, he was so outgoing, and we would have a lot of fun together.[13]

After Shippensburg, Lanza returned to New York, with a promise to contact Callinicos just as soon as he was needed. In fact, it would be another two years before the two men worked together again, for Lanza was about to embark on a major series of concert dates which would culminate in an appearance at the famed Hollywood Bowl, in Los Angeles. This was to be an appearance which would change for ever the planned course of his future career.

3   The Path Not Taken

When Columbia Artists approached Lanza with the idea of touring with a young soprano, Frances Yeend, for a select number of engagements which would take them across the United States, Canada, Newfoundland and Mexico, the tenor suggested that a third member be added to the team.

George London had also been a pupil of Rosati's, and possessed a superb bass-baritone voice which Lanza rightly felt would lend an added dimension to their programme of music. And a demanding and particularly felicitous programme of songs and arias it was too (see Stage, Radio and Television Appearances); professionally it was far removed from Lanza's repertoire in later years, when his immense popularity compelled him to concentrate on a more accessible, and less exacting, range of musical works.

The Bel Canto Trio, as they eventually came to be called, began their association with a concert in Milwaukee on 8 July 1947, and by the time they had sung their valedictory almost a year later, in Moncton, New Brunswick, they had become the most talked-about voices in American music circles. In a long and gruelling series of engagements which included stop-overs in places as diverse as Ames, Iowa and Minot, North Dakota, the trio laid the foundations for musical careers that would take them to some of the greatest opera houses in the world. Fortunately, given the close confines of the tour, the three singers were temperamentally well suited to one another. Indeed, the only problems which occurred during their year together, were those caused by Lanza's very real fear of flying. While London and Yeend happily took flights to whatever city happened to be next on the agenda, Lanza would insist on travelling by road or rail, often arriving at the concert hall with only minutes to spare. Still, it was the singing that mattered, and in this regard, the praise and adulation of critics and audiences alike was unstinting. And if Mario Lanza's name, in particular, was the one on every reviewer's lips, the other two didn't seem to mind very much.

Three young singers definitely on the way up ... Lanza was the most impressive of all, with the kind of voice that is needed to get all the drama out of such emotionally charged arias as 'E lucevan le stelle' and 'Celeste Aïda'.[1]

The favourite with the audience was the tenor, Lanza, a singer destined to enjoy a handsome career ... he has set up standards for himself and is eager to meet them. Clearly he is on his way ...[2]

By the time the trio had reached Chicago, for an open-air concert at the city's Grant Park, an audience of over 50,000 turned out to greet them. Claudia Cassidy, writing for the *Chicago Tribune*, completely lost her heart.

Young Mr Lanza was something approaching a sensation. You are a sensation in opera when customers whistle through their fingers and roar 'Bravo'. Mr Lanza sings for the indisputable reason that he was born to sing.[3]

Lanza's behaviour throughout the tour was exemplary, proving that when he was responsible to other performers, 'artistic temperament' was a term that simply didn't arise. Of the three, only George London was to achieve the success at places such as the Metropolitan which everyone at the time expected of Mario Lanza. Yet George London, in particular, would always maintain that in terms of pure, God-given vocal endowment, Lanza had no peer: 'If he could only have crawled out of his own skin and listened to his own voice, he might have lived his whole life differently.'[4]

None of the Bel Canto Trio's performances together were ever broadcast, although one recorded excerpt from *La Bohème* does survive. In April 1948, Lanza, Yeend and London were invited to perform part of Act 4 of Puccini's masterpiece, in English, before a specially invited audience at the NBC studios in Hollywood. The performance was the brainchild of the network's musical director, Peter Herman Adler, later to work with Lanza on *The Great Caruso*, and was aimed at convincing NBC chief David Sarnoff to give the green light to a proposed in-house opera company. It is a considerable testament to the skills of the three singers that Sarnoff immediately sanctioned the venture after the performance, although Lanza by now was destined to travel down a different road from that of his two contemporaries.

RCA Victor, meanwhile, were anxious to begin test recordings of the great voice and Lanza returned briefly to New York, where he cut a number of demonstration discs. One of these recordings eventually found its way to the offices of a woman named Ida Koverman, a noted patron of the arts who also happened to be personal secretary to Louis B. Mayer, legendary chief of the giant Metro-Goldwyn-Mayer film corporation. Once again the voice worked its magic. Mayer, in particular, was enthralled, and arrangements were made through Ida Koverman for an extra date to be added to Lanza's already burgeoning list of engagements. It was a date with a difference, however: a one-off concert at the movie capital's famed Hollywood Bowl, a vast open-air auditorium which boasted a superb acoustical setting in glorious natural surroundings. It would be Mario Lanza's two-hundreth concert appearance, and a significant turning point in his career.

The event took place on the evening of 28 August 1947, with the singers backed by a full symphony orchestra under the baton of Eugène Ormandy. As the main objective was to highlight Lanza's singing – a fact which made him unusually nervous before the performance – George London graciously agreed to join the audience out

front, leaving the stage to Lanza and Frances Yeend. MGM's rising young star, Kathryn Grayson, joined Mayer and Ida Koverman for the performance and the evening began with three solo arias from the tenor. By the time Frances Yeend joined him for a duet, the crowds were all but hoarse from cheering. They concluded their set with the love duet from *Madama Butterfly*, the sustained and thrilling climax to which brought the entire audience to its feet. Even George London was impressed: 'He sang that night like he had never sung before or has sung since.'[5]
It was an opinion universally echoed by the critics.

The sort of tenor voice that every operatic stage has been yearning for, lo these many lean years. Lanza's is the warm, round, typically Italian type of voice that caresses every graceful phrase and makes the listener breathe with him as it molds each curve of the melody.[6]

Electrified a large audience that cheered for several minutes ... He has truly a rare asset in a naturally beautiful voice, which he uses with intelligence, and a native artistry which, rightly developed, should prove his to be one of the exceptional voices of the generation.[7]

But if that appearance was the undoubted highlight of Mario Lanza's young career to date, it was also, conversely, its greatest tragedy. If he had been anything less than a sensation that evening, if the vocal magic had not been quite on target for the occasion, then Louis B. Mayer might well have walked away and forgotten all about him. But Louis B. Mayer stayed.

Louis B. Mayer was on his feet cheering with the rest of them, and mighty, all-powerful and unstoppable wheels in the MGM movie machine began slowly to grind into motion. In one important sense at least, the predicted future of the American Caruso was lost for ever in Hollywood that night. True, the Bel Canto Trio would continue to perform for some time yet, and there would even be two complete operatic performances on stage for the young tenor, but the combination of Mario Lanza's extraordinary talent, coupled with his almost total lack of high purpose and resolve, proved easy pickings for an organization as powerful and voracious as MGM. Warner Bros had the gangster movie, Universal had horror, but Metro-Goldwyn-Mayer was the undisputed home of the Hollywood musical, and Mario Lanza was about to become its newest and most popular star.

The audition which Lanza subsequently gave at MGM took place the day after the Hollywood Bowl concert – Mayer never being one to waste time – with Kathryn Grayson and some of the studio's top executives and producers in attendance. With his customary flair for the dramatic, Mayer insisted that the tenor be hidden behind a curtain, anxious initially to isolate the voice from the man. Lanza sang two numbers, 'Che gelida manina' from *La Bohème* and Victor Herbert's 'Thine Alone'. Mayer was convinced he had discovered the celluloid Caruso and it was a view shared by at least one of the producers present.

Joseph Pasternak, recently lured from Universal Pictures by Mayer, had the distinction of being the man who had previously groomed an unknown Deanna Durbin for stardom. He was soon to do the same for Mario Lanza.

> It was the most beautiful voice I had heard in my life and he [Mayer] said this is our new discovery. A few minutes later the curtain parted and out walked Mario Lanza ... bushy haired ... he looked like a caveman. And all the producers left ... I was the only one who stayed there. And I said to Mr Mayer, I'm going to do something because I liked his voice. And that's how it started.[8]

Things were now moving quickly – too quickly – for the 26-year-old tenor from south Philadelphia. At that time, Lanza had no intention of being sidetracked into a film career and indeed, his operatic debut was already being prepared. But with Betty now pregnant with their first child, the film company's offer was simply not to be resisted. He also believed it would be a one-off experience only; an opinion more than shared by some of Metro's senior executives, who couldn't see beyond the obvious obstacle of the tenor's bulging frame. With all this in mind, Sam Weiler was instructed to sit down with the company's lawyers and iron out a deal. To Lanza, it must have seemed an extraordinary arrangement. For signing a seven-year contract with the studio, he would immediately be paid a $10,000 bonus, with a further payment of $750 a week for six months while his first picture was being readied.

The remaining six months were given to him to do with as he pleased – concert or operatic appearances, recordings – whatever. Then, on the successful completion of his first film, he would be paid the sum of $15,000 which, if the picture proved popular, would be increased to $25,000 for his next one, and so on. Lanza couldn't believe his luck. As an additional gesture, MGM saw to it that Giacomo Spadoni, assistant chorus master of the Met in 1920 and confidant of Enrico Caruso, was engaged to work with him on the few operatic arias chosen for the film.

Spadoni let it be known to all and sundry that this was the greatest voice he had worked with since Caruso, and wisely took the time to caution his new protégé against the obvious temptations the movie capital had to offer. In the event, it wasn't hard to see why Lanza couldn't, or wouldn't, heed that advice to the full. Overnight he had gone from being a struggling unknown, as he saw it, to having a dream contract with one of the most prestigious studios in the world. To those who cautioned him against neglecting his operatic career, his reply was simple. On film, he maintained, he would bring classical music to more people worldwide than he could ever hope to do on the professional stage. It was a claim which would be repeated many times over in the years that followed, whenever the nagging question of his commitment to grand opera came up. And, on one level, it was a perfectly valid reply. Lanza did make the world of Puccini and his contemporaries far more accessible to a mass audience than the serious critics ever gave him credit for; but again, the eventual reper-cussions of that stance would undoubtedly take their toll on Mario Lanza's own opinion of his career.

None of this was even remotely considered in 1947 of

course, as Lanza took to the process of film-making with an enthusiasm that even the most hardened studio executives had to admire. With Pasternak as his mentor, Lanza submitted himself to the transformation process with an avid excitement and interest. The 'bushy hair' was the first thing to be corrected; the indignity of being taken to a ladies' hairdresser being short-lived when the tenor saw the results. Then there was the question of his weight.

Opera singers, especially tenors, are not generally noted for their slight build, and Mario Lanza was no exception. If he had stood at the excessive weight which would plague him in later years, Pasternak, and indeed MGM, might have baulked at taking him on, but all that Mario Lanza had to lose at that particular time in his career was a manageable 25 lb. It was all the more ironic that it was this very problem which led to his meeting Terry Robinson, the closest friend that Mario Lanza ever had in his short lifetime.

If Callinicos came to provide the backbone for the tenor's musical career, Robinson provided the greatest moral support away from the spotlight. A former Mr Universe who was known at MGM as the 'trainer to the stars', Terry Robinson was introduced to Lanza by Pasternak with strict instructions to get the boy into shape. Lanza had seen Robinson box in an amateur contest in Philadelphia several years earlier, and their mutual love of the sport helped seal a unique friendship which was to last throughout the tenor's life.

While Lanza's weight was being brought under control, screenwriters Bruce Manning and Tamara Hovey came up with a storyline which vaguely mirrored the tenor's own discovery by Koussevitsky. The film, *That Midnight Kiss*, was set in Philadelphia and had Lanza as a truck driver discovered singing while delivering a piano to the home of a wealthy patron of the arts. It was this particular aspect of the film which later gave rise to the popular notion that Lanza had been a piano mover when Koussevitsky had first heard him sing. But *That Midnight Kiss* was pure fiction from start to finish, with, for one thing,

Koussevitsky being replaced in the plot by Kathryn Grayson. Strong back-up was provided by such stalwarts as Ethel Barrymore, Keenan Wynn, J. Carroll Naish and pianist José Iturbi, and the whole film was brought together under the capable direction of Norman Taurog. Taurog, who later went on to direct a number of films with Elvis Presley, found in Lanza a co-operative and charming pupil – on their first outing together at least. For the score of the film, musical director Charles Previn and composer Bronislau Kaper came up with as wide a cross-section of music as possible to highlight the Lanza voice. From Jerome Kern's 'They Didn't Believe Me', an old Caruso favourite 'Mama mia che vo sape', and a new song specially written for the picture, 'I Know, I Know, I Know', the repertoire was light and relatively undemanding. Previn and lyricist William Katz also turned to Tchaikovsky for inspiration with two numbers, 'One Love of Mine' taken from the famous Piano Concerto in B Flat Minor (later dropped from the finished picture) and 'Love is Music', a souped-up adaptation of the main theme from the Fifth Symphony, which Lanza and Grayson sing at the close of the film. But it was the picture's operatic excerpts, or rather one in particular, which set the final seal on Mario Lanza's career in Hollywood.

With the brief exception of a snippet of 'Una furtiva lagrima', the tenor's sole operatic contribution came in the form of a spirited rendition of the ever-popular 'Celeste Aïda', even then denied the recitative introduction, 'Se quel guerrier io fossi ...', by a studio still wary of the commercial appeal of opera on film. In the event, it proved to be the single most popular scene with preview audiences when the film was screened on its completion.

The aria is introduced in a concert sequence in the film by José Iturbi and it is not hard today to see why those subsequent few on-screen minutes made such an impact with audience and critics alike. All that Mario Lanza represented at that time in his life is there to be seen: the dark, Italianate good looks, the boyish charm and uncomplicated appeal, and the fresh, gloriously natural tenor voice, the sound of which had never before graced the silver screen. It would take Lanza another two films and one particular recording before he would become an undisputed super star, but by the completion of *That Midnight Kiss*, he was already well on his way.

While the picture was being readied, Lanza undertook his professional operatic debut with the New Orleans Opera House Association, as Pinkerton, in two performances of Puccini's *Madama Butterfly*, at the Municipal Auditorium in St Louis. Soprano Tomiko Kanazawa sang the role of Butterfly, and in a review of 9 April 1948, critic Laurence Oden wrote:

> Mario Lanza performed his duties as Lieut. Pinkerton with considerable verve and dash. Rarely have we seen a more superbly romantic leading tenor. His exceptionally beautiful voice helps immeasurably – the combination of good looks and vocal ability should prove most helpful to Mr Lanza in any of his more earnest undertakings.[9]

The fact that *Madama Butterfly* is not a 'tenor's' opera often gave rise to claims in later years that Lanza was unable to sustain a full role in some of the more demanding works, but the choice of such a lightweight part had as much to do with his looks as it did his singing. With Terry Robinson's help, and the sort of financial incentives that MGM had on offer, the usually heavy tenor had slimmed down to his lowest weight in years – both visually and vocally, he was now the perfect leading man for opera and films. The dashing Lieutenant Pinkerton was an ideal role and the film studios would have him reprise the famous love duet in his next picture, *The Toast of New Orleans*, which was already being prepared on the strength of the studio rushes of *That Midnight Kiss*.

Sadly however, those two performances as Pinkerton in New Orleans would remain the only occasion when the Lanza voice would grace a full length operatic production. Plans were forever being made and cancelled for that long-awaited return engagement, literally up to the day of Lanza's death, but it was not to be, and, as we will see, the reasons had nothing whatever to do with any shortcomings in the tenor's vocal abilities. Lanza himself remained adamant on the subject: 'As an opera singer I'm still a baby twenty-seven. Give me eight more years. Then we will see.'[10]

Following the New Orleans engagement, Lanza returned to Hollywood, where he and Betty moved into a palatial home on Whittier Drive, in Beverly Hills. It was the first real taste of the sweet life for both of them, further blessed by the birth of their first child, Colleen, on 9 December that year.

MGM, meanwhile, set about promoting their new star in a series of carefully planned appearances throughout the country. With his commitments to the Bel Canto Trio now at an end, the studio quickly arranged a return engagement at the Hollywood Bowl on 24 July 1948, this time with co-star Kathryn Grayson in support. Following more work at MGM, a community concert tour with twenty-seven dates was put together for the tenor by Columbia Artists, this time highlighting his talents as a solo performer. It would prove to be the very last time that Mario Lanza would appear in public as a 'serious' concert artist; the subsequent successes of his film and recording career moved him into an entirely different category altogether.

Lanza's promise two years earlier to re-engage Callinicos had not been forgotten, and the two men prepared for a tour which would take them to some of the lesser known concert venues across the United States. But if the voice had improved in the intervening years, Callinicos soon noticed another, more disturbing trend manifest itself on the tour.

> We opened with a cancellation in Bluefield, West Virginia, and closed with a cancellation in Lincoln, Nebraska. Out of 27 dates, Mario was on hand for 12. He ducked out of some dates without giving a reason. For others, he pleaded a cold – 'pneumonia' he insisted on calling it. Sensing his imminent rise as a screen personality ... Mario was disturbed as a petulant child at the prospect of playing the 'tank' towns for so little money. Already he had notions

about singing in the big cities for top fees. Mario had a case
of swollen pride well in advance of success.[11]

The tour was not without its happy moments though, as
Costa later recalled.

> One of our concerts took place in Zanesville, Ohio. The
> Community Concerts have people who are the hosts to
> meet the artists at the train, and also after the concert the
> next day. So this nice elderly couple picked us up at the
> hotel and they were driving us to the railroad station and
> on the way, the lady said 'Mr Lanza, how do you like our
> city?' and naturally we loved Zanesville very much ... And
> then she said, 'You know Mr Lanza and Mr Callinicos, you
> should come back to Zanesville in the Spring to see the
> daffodils grow, because they are beautiful in the Spring ...'
> and Mario looked at me and winked and said, 'We're sure
> gonna come back in the Spring to see the daffodils'. And
> that remained a standing joke between us, because
> whether we were in Scotland, in Glasgow, or in Germany,
> in Hamburg or Kiel, Mario would say to me 'Hey Costa,
> you know something? We forgot to go to Zanesville to see
> the daffodils. But we'll do it next Spring ...'[12]

For Callinicos, that simple, uncomplicated time in
Zanesville would always represent something of a
watershed in their professional life together: a time of
innocence that would never come again.

4 *Super Star*

At the conclusion of the community concert tour, Lanza returned once more to New York, where he began preparations for his recording debut with RCA Victor. Jean Paul Morel of the New York City Opera was engaged to conduct for the session, which was scheduled to take place at the Manhattan Center on 5 May 1949. Things, however, did not go quite as planned.

Unlike Callinicos, Morel had no experience of the tenor's unpredictable behaviour, and when the two began rehearsing at the New York City Opera studio, the conductor, understandably, saw it as his job to correct Lanza when he saw fit. It was a wrong move on Morel's part, however well intentioned. 'Correcting' Mario Lanza, even at that early stage of his career, was simply not on. Lanza walked out, informing RCA that he would attend the session only if his friend, Costa Callinicos, were allowed to conduct. Not surprisingly, RCA were reluctant to entrust the recording to a relative unknown, and with less than five hours to prepare for it, even Callinicos was nervous. But Lanza stood firm and the booking went ahead as planned. Two arias and two Neapolitan songs were chosen and that pattern of recording – four songs to a session – would remain a standard with Lanza throughout his career. With rare exceptions, such as a number of ill-judged productions in Rome, ten years later, the practice set down that day in 1949 never varied.

With RCA's top A & R (artist and repertoire) man Richard Mohr in charge of production, Lanza produced a remarkably accomplished and confident body of work, completing all four selections in single 'takes'. One of the numbers, the *Bohème* aria 'Che gelida manina', was subsequently voted operatic recording of the year by the National Record Critics Association, and was also added to RCA's prestigious 'Hall of Fame' catalogue of historical performances. With only a few exceptions, Lanza would maintain that high standard of work throughout his recording career, although there would be times, particularly during a number of 'one-take' sessions, when a little more attention to some of the music's finer points would undoubtedly have resulted in a better quality of performance. But that was Mario Lanza, as Mohr recalled:

> The magnificence didn't change. The problem was one of energy. When Mario was heavy he felt he could sing as much as he wanted, so he would do numerous 'takes' for us. When he was thin, one 'take' was all he would do. The orchestra was always well rehearsed and we got spontaneous performances from Lanza. Either way he was fine – it was just that he was more comfortable heavy.[1]

The session on 5 May also marked Callinicos's recording debut as a conductor, a role which despite the lack of advance preparation, he handled beautifully. Afterwards, he and Lanza posed together for a photograph, the tenor holding the song sheet to 'Mama mia che vo sape'. 'Now we are down for posterity, Costas,' he said, and a great, if at times undisciplined, recording career was born.

Lanza's promotion of *That Midnight Kiss* began in earnest with the film's completion in 1949. As part of the promotional campaign, Lanza made his third and final appearance at the Hollywood Bowl, at yet another 'Salute to MGM' spectacular. Eleanor Powell danced, André Previn played, Carmen Miranda sang, and with composer Johnny Green conducting for the tenor, Lanza treated the audience to a thrilling 'Celeste Aïda' – which also happened to be featured in *That Midnight Kiss*'. The film was eventually released in the spring of 1949 and proved, yet again, that when it came to predicting the tastes of the movie-going public, Louis B. Mayer couldn't be faulted. His 'Gable-with-a-voice' was an overnight sensation, and

any plans that Mario Lanza might have had for an alternative career in grand opera were now definitely on hold.

As for the budding Mr Lanza, the opinion rendered of him
by the sanguine Mr Iturbi is good enough for us. 'His
voice,' says Mr Iturbi, 'has quality and warmth, and he has
a very nice personality.' Check! Maybe he isn't a new
Caruso, as they claim him to be, but then, who is?[2]

With both MGM and RCA vying for his time, Lanza spent
the remainder of 1949 dividing his talent between the
recording studios in New York and the soundstages of
Hollywood. For his next picture, *The Toast of New Orleans*,
screenwriters Sy Gomberg and George Wells came up
with yet another paper-thin plot, this time revolving
around a New Orleans fisherman with a magnificent
voice, who goes on to become a great opera star. Lanza's
co-stars were Kathryn Grayson and J. Carroll Naish again,
and, somewhat surprisingly, the quietly debonair David
Niven, whose own career was in something of a slump at
the time. Niven was prepared to take work wherever he
could find it, even in a Mario Lanza musical, but despite
the obvious differences in their respective backgrounds,
the two men got on exceptionally well throughout the
filming. Indeed, it could be said that the only people who
were beginning to find Lanza difficult to handle were the
studio executives. Lanza's old problems with authority
were beginning to surface again and it was on the set of
The Toast of New Orleans that the first real indications of the
troubles ahead became evident. Occasional outbursts of
hostility toward his employers were, in his mind,
constantly outweighed by his consideration for the lesser
paid employees on the set. Many a time a take would be
deliberately fluffed by the tenor, so that the scene would
have to be re-shot the following day, with all the resulting
overtime going to an increasingly grateful crew of
technicians and extras.

In addition, he was eating and drinking too much, and it
soon became obvious that the studio's main concern was
with its star's ever-expanding waistline. Lanza's appetite
for food was indeed prodigious, prompting Pasternak at

one stage to appoint a guardian to ensure that no secret meals were smuggled on to the set for the tenor during filming. The stories of these occasional eating binges – some real, most of them exaggerated – found themselves into print on countless occasions in the years that followed, proving a constant and very real source of annoyance to Lanza wherever he went. Depending on which account the gullible reader was prepared to believe, Mario Lanza was capable of consuming twenty-three baby chickens – or twenty-three 'pieces' of chicken – at a single sitting, usually washed down by anywhere between fifteen and twenty bottles of Coca Cola. Terry Robinson had come on to the Lanza payroll and did what he could to keep the singer in shape, but it wasn't always easy.

Mario Lanza was born big. A fifty-inch chest. For films they wanted him small. He would go up and down. When Mario Lanza drank a glass of water, he would gain three pounds. If I drank that same glass, I wouldn't gain anything. Mario Lanza, when he was frustrated, when he was upset – he was super, super sensitive – would eat. We couldn't stop him, because when I tried, he would eat. twice as much ... go behind my back like a little baby. He was uncontrollable at these times, but that was his problem and basically he punished himself without punishing other people. But Mario was born big. His neck size was 19, his sleeve length 36½ inches. That's a big man.[3]

But heavy or thin, Mario Lanza could still sing like no man alive and it was this, his second picture, which finally confirmed his status as an entertainer of world renown. The popular numbers chosen for the film were staged by musical director George Stoll, a previous Oscar winner for his work on the classic Gene Kelly musical *Anchors Aweigh* 1945. Stoll was a great admirer of the Lanza voice and would go on to work on all but two of the tenor's future pictures. In *The Toast of New Orleans*, both men had a rich and varied selection of music to work with.

Earlier, in New York, Lanza had been introduced to yet another of Joe Pasternak's discoveries, a Hungarian-born *émigré* by the name of Nicholas Brodszky, a composer who was keen to write for the tenor. With the singer's second film, he was given his chance and, along with lyricist Sammy Cahn, came up with five new songs for the picture. Both 'I'll Never Love You' and 'The Bayou Lullaby' were ballads in the classical tradition, while 'The Tina Lina' and 'Boom Biddy Boom Boom' – admittedly not Sammy Cahn's finest work – were novelty songs all put over with gusto and style by Lanza's robust singing. But it was Brodszky's fifth song, a 'love theme for Mario Lanza', that finally did the trick.

> Joe Pasternak called me one day to come over and meet composer Nicholas Brodszky. Brodszky had patent leather hair and the kind of shape that if you pushed him over, he would roll back up – which is good if you're going to compose. On the piano, he had a printed sheet of music – not a hand-written manuscript, but printed. No chance of changing a note with this man! It was titled 'Love Theme for Mario Lanza'. Could I write words for it? they asked. I started to write and what gradually came out was:
> 'Be my love, for no one else can end this yearning,
> This need that you and you alone create …'
> Now if you've only heard Mr Lanza on a record or a tape, you've never heard him at all, because no mechanical reproduction could capture the startling brilliance of that voice. It scared the hell out of you. I believe he had a soft pedal and a loud pedal in his throat.[4]

It would be an understatement to say that Mario Lanza's recording of 'Be My Love' in 1950 was a sensation. It was more than that. Much more. Its soaring melody line and romantic lyric could have suited almost any singer alive – from Sinatra to Crosby, Deanna Durbin to Judy Garland – but for a classically trained singer like Lanza to do with it what he did, that, quite simply, had never been done before.

The musical bridge between Verdi on the one hand, and somebody like Cole Porter on the other, is immense – the one demanding a singer's full vocal commitment, the other only half – and cross-overs between the two were seldom successfully ventured. When an operatically trained voice occasionally did attempt the leap, the results could at best be described as charming; the formality of the reading often won out over a more emotive interpretation and understanding of the lyric. Then too, 'accent' was always a problem. Before Lanza, there were few American tenors of note who strayed into main-stream, popular music and it was left to the likes of Gigli (an Italian), Kiepura (a Pole) or Tauber (an Austrian) to get to grips, often uneasily, with music more suited to Sinatra or Crosby.

Lanza however, was in a different class entirely. If his operatic recordings were never as musically polished as those of some of his peers in that particular medium, he more than compensated in terms of sheer versatility. He was a 'romantic' singer of the very first order, and while enthusiasts might marvel at the tenor of di Stefano or Bjoerling, they fell in love with the voice of Mario Lanza. It was as real and as simple as that, and following the release of *The Toast of New Orleans*, sales of 'Be My Love' took off like no other record before it.

In no time at all, it seemed, the whole world had 'Lanza fever', and if the serious critics were by now throwing up their hands in despair at the careless abuse of a mighty talent, Lanza could hardly be blamed for not taking too much notice.

As well as including the romantic melodies of Brodszky and Cahn, the producers of *The Toast of New Orleans* were also more adventurous in the use of operatic excerpts throughout the film. Admittedly, these excerpts were still mainstream popular arias, but at least this type of music was being presented to a mass audience who clearly wanted more. The picture concluded with a lengthy excerpt from *Madama Butterfly* staged by composer Johnny Green and magnificently sung on screen by Lanza and Kathryn Grayson. In later years, Lanza's singing was often described as having 'animal magnetism', and the description stems from this particular scene. The sheer vitality of Lanza's singing comes across as vibrantly today as it did back in 1950. All of those things which made his operatic singing so appealing to a mass audience are there in those moments – the almost absurd self-confidence, the brashness, the good looks, and the fabulous, ringing tenor voice. Kathryn Grayson was beautiful to behold, but it was Lanza, and how he looked and sang, who held the attention. 'Star quality' is often difficult to define, but MGM's new super star had it by the cart load – and no one knew it better than Mario Lanza himself.

The tenor's recording of 'Be My Love' took place at Republic Studios in Hollywood on 27 June 1950. The orchestration this time was given over to Ray Sinatra, first cousin to Frank, and the man who would alternate with Callinicos in conducting for Lanza in the immediate years ahead. Generally speaking, Sinatra would conduct for the tenor's popular recordings, while Costa would handle the classical selections. Lanza himself was entirely pleased with this arrangement, and it would not be until 1955 – over half-way through his entire recording career – that he would find time to work with someone other than these two men in the studio. By now too, Callinicos was on a retainer, and any vocal workouts undertaken by Lanza were done under his supervision. But it was under Sinatra's direction that he achieved his first gold record, over one and a half million copies sold at a time when the industry was not geared for the kind of hype which governs it today. It was an additional bonus for Lanza too. As a Red Seal, or classical recording artist for RCA, he was entitled to 10 per cent more of the record's profits than his popular song contemporaries.

'Be My Love' eventually came to be regarded as Mario Lanza's theme song, and it was used as the introductory number to his weekly series of radio shows which began the following year. In the space of two short years, Lanza had gone from being practically unknown, to being a super star, with the ability to make the sort of fortunes that even Sam Weiler never dreamed of. It was an overnight success story on the grandest scale, and with it came the seeds of the singer's eventual downfall, as Joe Pasternak, for one, was soon to learn.

Success is harder to take than failure. He was not equipped to be very successful and overnight he became the sensation of the world. I don't think he could take it. He came to me one day with a cheque for $1,100,000 royalties from his recordings. You know if a man didn't have $10 and you get a cheque like that, very few of them could stay sober.[5]

Pasternak meant it figuratively as well as literally, of course, but if the tenor could disguise his occasional drinking excesses, his problems with over-eating were becoming increasingly obvious. By the time *The Toast of New Orleans* had been completed, he tipped the scales at over 200 lb. More demands than ever were now being made on the Caruso with the movie-star looks, and this, along with the difficulties encountered in shedding the pounds, had a further destabilizing effect on his already volatile personality. Lanza became 'difficult' to handle and the press fairly soaked it up.

But if a war of sorts was being waged by Mario Lanza to control those temperamental excesses, his associates in the recording studios had nothing but praise for his singing. Many consider him to have been at the peak of his powers during this period of his life, and listening today to some of those famous 'takes', it is difficult not to agree: a blistering, definitive, one-take recording of 'Granada', with Sinatra; a tender, expressive 'Virgin's Slumber Song', with Costa, and an adaptation of Gerda Bielenberg's 'Guardian Angels', set to music by no less a talent than Harp Marx.

Lanza also returned to the concert platform, briefly, in the spring of 1950 although the attraction of the venue chosen for the occasion – Hawaii – may have had more to do with his decision to sing than any more serious commitment.

On 3 December 1950, Betty gave birth to the Lanza's second child, Ellisa, and with the tenor in as relaxed a state of mind as it was ever possible for him to be in, the stage was now set for his greatest triumph: the ultimate tribute to his idol, which would also turn Mario Lanza from a super star into a legend.

*

In terms of artistic output on film, in concert and on records, the years 1951 to mid-1952 were by far the most satisfyingly prodigious in Mario Lanza's brief career. Everything he touched at that time turned to gold. In his acting, as well as his singing, the challenges put before him were there simply for the savouring. If he gave the impression that vocally he could do or sing just about anything, it was probably because he well-nigh could. The range and flexibility of shadings in his voice seemed to attain a fusion of just about everything it took to make it perfect: dazzling top notes, the depth and breadth of which have seldom been equalled, effortlessly supported by a satin-smooth lower register.

No matter what type of music was presented to him, Lanza approached each selection with the same joyous intensity of performance; he set a standard of singing, moreover, which seemed to imbue even the most mediocre of numbers with a warmth and spontaneity far beyond the apparent demands of the song. He was very much the 'tenor-as-super star' supreme, and if, as has often been claimed, his ego tended to expand with his glamorous lifestyle, the reasons were obvious to all. With his weight at least controllable, the movie-star looks which went with the voice made for a devastating combination of talent and charm.

He was ready now, to undertake the role which many felt he had subconsciously been preparing for all his life; a role, furthermore, which would ensure Mario Lanza a lasting place in the annals of great Hollywood musicals and would link for ever the two greatest voices of the century. That said, however, the idea of casting Mario Lanza in the title role of the great Caruso came not from Mayer, or Pasternak, or anyone else at MGM for that matter. It came instead from another great pioneer of the film industry, Jesse L. Lasky, founder member of Famous-Players Lasky Corporation – later Paramount Pictures – and the man who had produced the few excursions into silent pictures by Enrico Caruso several decades earlier.

Now over seventy, Lasky was in virtual retirement, but

the idea of filming Caruso's life story had been a dream nurtured for many years. It seemed an impossible dream at times, for even Lasky had begun to doubt the likelihood of ever finding someone to fill the demands of the mighty role. Then, with Lanza, everything changed almost overnight. He had the looks, the voice, and the box-office pull to maybe, just maybe, produce the sort of tribute that would appeal to opera lovers and movie-goers alike. Lasky decided to act, and when he approached Mayer with a proposal to join in as executive producer on the project, he found in him, at least, an enthusiastic supporter. The studio executives, on the other hand, were less sure. For one thing, television was beginning to make huge inroads on the film company's profits in the early 1950s, and Lanza's proven box-office record notwithstanding, the idea of producing what would be tantamount to an all-opera film was understandably viewed with more than a degree of scepticism by the corporate body.

Then too, Louis B. Mayer's days as head of the giant corporation were coming to a close and he would soon be replaced by Dore Schary, a no-nonsense businessman whose attitude to temperamental stars would eventually result in one of the great studio stand-offs in Hollywood's colourful history. But that was further down the road, for in early 1950, when Mario Lanza first got word of the Caruso project and the problems surrounding it, there was little portent of the disasters that lay ahead. His immediate reaction was to telephone Mayer and place his full support behind the production. With Lasky engaged as executive producer, *The Great Caruso* was eventually given the green light, and while William Ludwig and Sonya Levien got together to fashion a screenplay 'suggested' by Dorothy Caruso's biography of her husband, Lanza embarked on the most committed period of training he would ever undertake for a motion picture.

The weight was the first problem to be brought under control, and the tenor rented Ginger Rogers's ranch in Medford, Oregon, for a six-week training programme supervised by Terry Robinson, who was now living with the family. The Lanza entourage also consisted of Betty, their two children, a butler, a cook, and Jack Keller, the singer's press agent, who was there simply to deal with the flood of offers which were rolling in daily. The regimen of exercises prepared by Terry Robinson – the skimpy meals, the roadwork, the weightlifting – was torture for Lanza but by the end of six weeks, he had lost almost 40 lb off his bulging frame and felt fitter and happier than he had in years. He was now set to embark on the performance of his career: the ultimate and supreme tribute to the man, the singer, who had inspired him more than any other.

In preparing for the role of Enrico Caruso, Lanza adopted what today would be seen as an exemplary approach to the part. For the eight weeks of actual shooting and the few weeks of preparatory work that went into it, Lanza *was* Caruso: dressing like him, studying his walk and mannerisms from old movie and newsreel footage, and most of all, listening over and over again to the master's recordings.

It was an idea ahead of its time, for instead of praising him for his efforts, the press began to wonder if he wasn't taking the whole idea a bit too far. *Confidential*, the notorious gossip magazine, even went so far as to headline a story 'Is Mario Lanza Looney?', hardly the most flattering comment on an approach which today would be worthy of a de Niro or Hoffman. But for once, Lanza wasn't to be swayed, and by his efforts, he managed to produce the most natural and affecting performance he would ever give on screen. Some credit too, of course, must be given to director Richard Thorpe, but in truth, it was Lanza's determination to honour his idol in the best possible way that ultimately produced the result.

Ludwig and Levien's screenplay was very much a Hollywood version of Caruso's life, which is to say that anything dull or even remotely unsavoury was simply never allowed to appear. Little surprise then, that the singer's first common-law wife and their two sons were never even mentioned. It was a classic case of 'when the facts interfere with the legend, print the legend', as John Ford put it, albeit in a different context.

Lanza's overnight success had also not impressed the

more serious-minded critics, who understandably felt that
the singer had still a long way to go before he could even
hope to fill Caruso's shoes. It was an opinion shared too,
by Dorothy Caruso, who knew, more than most, the long
gruelling years and heavy toll in health paid by her
husband in achieving what he did. She had little regard in
the end, for *The Great Caruso*, and the film's highly
romanticized story-telling did not alter her opinion.

But in all other respects, Lanza did do an enormous
service to his illustrious predecessor. For the musical
scoring of the film, Johnny Green was put in charge of the
few popular numbers, while at Lanza's insistence, Peter
Herman Adler took control of the operatic selections. In
all, over twenty-one songs and arias were highlighted,
with the tenor receiving impressive back-up from soloists
and chorus members of the Metropolitan. Dorothy
Kirsten, Blanche Thebom, Nicola Moscona, Giuseppe
Valdengo and Gilbert Russell all gave thrilling support
to the Lanza voice, and under Adler's expert guidance,
the tenor produced some of his finest operatic singing
ever.

The film successfully recalled the Caruso years with
superb renditions of some of the great man's most popular
arias: with 'La Donna e mobile', 'Che gelida manina' and
that 'lucky' aria, 'Vesti la giubba' being particularly
outstanding. Lanza's singing style was very much his own
and it was that vocal openness, that expansive way with a
song, that helped secure the film's lasting success.

His peers from the Metropolitan, Peter Herman Adler in
particular, were among the first to recognize the
extraordinary appeal and quality of the voice.

> He had what Caruso had ... the most brilliant, natural,
> broad voice without limitation ... and he had a natural
> peasant aggressiveness, which is so good in the Caruso
> recordings, because what the Caruso recordings made
> famous was not the quality of the voice, but this vitality,
> this tremendous vitality, and that Mario absolutely had.
> And he really would have become, what already his

neighbours in south Philadelphia say of him, an American Caruso.[6]

In addition to the operatic excerpts featured in the film, bandleader Irving Aaronson and lyricist Paul Francis Webster contributed a new song, 'The Loveliest Night of the Year', which was sung on screen by Lanza's co-star, Ann Blyth. The song was an adaptation of the popular standard, 'Over the Waves', and following the tenor's own recording of the number in New York, in 1951, it went on to become his second million-selling single.

The Great Caruso opened in May 1951, at New York's Radio City Music Hall, the world's largest cinema auditorium, where it broke all previous box-office records at the theatre and eventually earned its volatile star over three million dollars from receipts and recording royalties alone.

Not surprisingly, the critics were lavish with their praise:

Lanza dominates the whole screen when his commanding voice sings the great arias.[7]

Lanza's young tenor voice is unusual and he sings with remarkable dramatic strength.[8]

Lanza has a handsome, becoming appearance, his voice reminiscent of the rare magnificence of the lyrical emotions expressed by Caruso. He comes astonishingly close to the original.[9]

It was nothing short of a 'Lanza Bonanza', as Terry Robinson liked to put it, and even Caruso's own recordings started selling well again – an additional bonus for RCA, who recorded both singers.

Away from the film's soundstages, Lanza had recorded a number of popular arias with Callinicos, and eight of these were quickly put together for an LP titled *The Great Caruso*. No matter that only four of the arias chosen were actually featured in the film: it was seen as the official soundtrack album and sales quickly topped 100,000, a feat hitherto unheard of for a classical collection. It would eventually sell over one million copies and in doing so, become the first operatic LP to go gold.

Lanza was unstoppable. Columbia Artists could hardly deal with the offers coming in from concert venues across the country. Because of the pressure of work the tenor now found himself under, a planned operatic appearance in *Andrea Chenier* with diva Renata Tebaldi at the San Francisco Opera House had to be called off. That particular production eventually went ahead with the Italian tenor Mario del Monaco making his American debut. But a 22-city concert tour in February/March 1951 was agreed with Lanza's management team and it turned out to be the single most spectacular conquest of a mass audience by any performer at that time. Even Callinicos was surprised by the reaction to the man and his voice.

> If you had seen and heard what went on in 22 cities from Scranton, Pennsylvania to Fresno, California … you would have understood the ambivalent attitudes performers have to their public. I was there. I saw it, I heard it. I was touched by it and almost maimed by it from time to time. And mind, my name was not Mario Lanza.[10]

Lanza had unleashed the sort of fan adulation normally reserved for popular, mainstream entertainers. And he had done this by singing, for the most part, operatic and classical songs. If the audiences attending those concerts expected a light selection of popular ballads and movie tunes, the actual programme presented by the tenor must have come as a considerable surprise:

'Lamento di Federica' from *L'Arlesiana* by Cilea
'Gia il sole del gange' by Scarlatti
'Pieta Signore' by Stradella
'The House on the Hill' by Ernest Charles
'Bonjour ma belle' by Behrend
'Vesti la giubba' from *Pagliacci* by Leoncavallo

After the intermission, Lanza concluded his concert with:

'Marechiare' by Tosti
'A' Vuchella' also by Tosti
'La Danza' by Rossini
'Softly as in a Morning Sunrise' by Romberg
'I'm Falling in Love with Someone' by Victor Herbert.

In addition, Callinicos played several solos throughout, providing breaks which only helped heighten the audience anticipation for Lanza's return to stage. The inevitable encores usually included 'Be My Love' and 'La Donna e mobile', with 'Because' thrown in for good measure. Callinicos provided piano accompaniment throughout the tour except for one or two occasions when the singer was backed by a full symphony orchestra. One was scheduled for the evening of 6 March at the Syria Mosque, in Pittsburgh.

As tickets for the entire tour had been sold out weeks in advance, Lanza was persuaded for this particular date to allow the management to sell seats for his afternoon rehearsal with conductor Vladimir Bakaleinikoff. Edward Specter, manager of the Pittsburgh Symphony, promptly placed an advertisement in the morning newspapers:

> Due to the fact that the Pittsburgh Symphony Concert on Tuesday evening, March 6th, with Mario Lanza as soloist has been completely booked out, and because of the continued and overwhelming demand for tickets, the rehearsal for the concert will be open to the public at general admission prices.[11]

The rehearsal was sold out within hours, although 'rehearsal' is perhaps too refined a word for what took place that afternoon. When Lanza sang, all was quiet; an adoring audience hung on to his every phrase. When he was not singing, however, complete pandemonium broke out. 'Be My Love, Mario ...', 'Sing Because ...' – it was impossible to control them and equally impossible for Lanza and the orchestra to attend properly to the task in hand. Bakaleinikoff was furious, stopping the orchestra at one point to shout 'Shut up!' to the unruly crowd. The audience on the night of the concert were better behaved, but the cheers, as always, seemed to go on forever, a fact not lost on the reviewer in the *Pittsburgh Press* the following day:

> Mario Lanza and the Pittsburgh Symphony Orchestra rocked the Syria Mosque last night until the building itself blew a fuse or something. The Mosque was packed for the event. About the only place you didn't see a face was in the huge chandelier suspended above the auditorium. And we are not quite sure of that place either. For when you jam 4,000 people into the Mosque, you are jamming. But jammed or not the auditorium cheered, and cheered and cheered and each went home singing 'Be My Love' after their own fashion. That's about the time the lights went out ...[12]

It was the same wherever they went, from the spectacle of 10,000 screaming fans in Omaha, Nebraska, to a slightly more refined audience at the Philadelphia Academy of Music, where Koussevitsky had first heard Lanza sing, a whole lifetime ago. Amazingly, there were no cancellations, no temper tantrums and no walkouts. He also watched what he ate, making sure that the appearance was always in harmony with the voice.

> Slimmed down, vigorous and athletic in his manner, elegantly attired in dark blue suit, black form-fitting overcoat, gray Homburg, blue tie with gold stripes, black shoes, gray socks, gray gloves, gray muffler, Mario would have been attractive in any crowd. With the voice at center stage, he was truly magnificent.[13]

It was the Caruso tour, and the happiest, most uncomplicated period in his life.

Among the many offers coming Lanza's way was one from the Coca Cola Corporation, who wanted him for his own weekly radio programme, *The Mario Lanza Show*. Lanza accepted, and fifty-nine programmes in all were broadcast on CBS and NBC between 26 June 1951 and 22

August 1952. It was a happy decision all round, with the subsequent recordings providing a dazzling legacy of magnificent Lanza performances in the years to come. At that particular time though, no one intended that recordings of any of the performances would be commercially released. That decision would come, of necessity, at a later date, when the tenor's legal battles with the studio would temporarily prevent him from recording. It was originally planned that the show would be taped before a 'live' audience, but scenes such as those at Pittsburgh caused a serious re-think on the matter and it was eventually decided instead to add an 'applause' track after each take, thus allowing Lanza complete freedom in the studio to run through the numbers as often as he liked.

The format of the weekly show featured four selections from Lanza, two from a guest artist – usually the popular Canadian singer Giselle MacKenzie – and two orchestral settings from Ray Sinatra. Callinicos was also engaged as assistant leader of the orchestra, and while subsequent record releases from these sessions always credit Sinatra with conducting for Lanza, rehearsal outtakes clearly show that Costa took charge on many of the numbers. Generally speaking, Sinatra would conduct for the popular ballads while Callinicos would take care of the operatic and Neapolitan song selections. As for Lanza's singing, it was nothing less than inspired. On those weekly programmes he covered virtually the entire spectrum of vocal styles: from Cole Porter to Puccini, from Romberg to Tosti, and he somehow managed to do it all without ever once breaking vocal stride.

A case in point was the selection for the night of 9 September 1951. From Porter's romantic classic 'Night and Day' to Grieg's 'I Love Thee', Romberg's 'The Desert Song' and on through to the great *Tosca* aria 'E lucevan le stelle', it was a range of singing styles which would have intimidated the most seasoned professional. To Mario Lanza though, it was all good music, all worthy of his fullest commitment and effort.

It was more than good enough. Virtually the entire American popular songbook was covered – although he never did get to sing Gershwin – with old standards such as 'Song of Songs' or 'A Little Love, A Little Kiss' sounding as they never had before, or ever would again. As Callinicos observed: 'When he sang a song or aria, Mario sounded as if someone had told him, this is going to be the last singing you're going to do on this earth. As if it were going to be that last thing, that's what he brought with the pronunciation of the words, with the phrasing, and with the warmth and knowledge that his recordings show.'[14]

Mario Lanza was just thirty years old, immensely wealthy and, it could be argued, the most popular operatic tenor in the world. If unconditional critical acclaim for the type of singing he loved best would always elude him, he must also have realized that however great his natural talent undoubtedly was, true greatness as an opera singer could only come with years of self-discipline and study. It was Lanza's decision therefore, and his alone, to stay where he was, and even in later years, in Rome, when his film career had waned considerably, he still refused to commit himself to the stage. It was always 'next year'. Next year I'll sing at La Scala, or Covent Garden, or the Rome Opera House, or wherever ... until there were no more 'next years' left to come. In a sense, Lanza saw himself as 'the people's tenor'. The old excuse of bringing opera to the masses was trotted out again and again until even he himself began to believe it. All the temper tantrums, all the unpredictable outbursts were reserved solely for those in authority.

To his friends, and all those 'little people' who could never expect to be heard above the crowd, he showed extreme kindness and consideration. A case in point was his friendship with a ten-year-old child, Raphaela Fasano, from Newark, New Jersey. In 1951, when Mario Lanza could claim to be the most popular movie-star in America, it must have seemed inconceivable that ordinary people could gain an audience with the American Caruso. Yet these were the very people Lanza chose to have around him and if his in-built resentment towards authority figures helped, in no small way, to blind him to the more opportunistic motives of some alleged 'friends' and

The Merry Wives of Windsor, Tanglewood, 7 August 1942. Lanza
is on the extreme left

Tenor triumphant – at the Hollywood
Bowl, 28 August 1947

With Giselle MacKenzie during rehearsals
for *The Mario Lanza Show*, 1951

With Richard Mohr at a
RCA recording session,
Manhattan Centre,
New York,
23 February 1951

Recording for RCA Victor, Manhattan Centre, New York,
23 February 1951

Raphaela Fasano with Mario Lanza at a Hollywood Party, 1951

Scene from *For the First Time*
with Mario Lanza as Radames

The Great Caruso

Madama Butterfly duet
with Kathryn Grayson
from *The Toast of New Orleans*

A serenade for the fans on Victoria Station, London,
14 November 1957

Mario Lanza with his wife and four children on the Warner Bros. set during the filming of *Serenade*, 1955

With Terry Robinson at MGM Studios, 1952

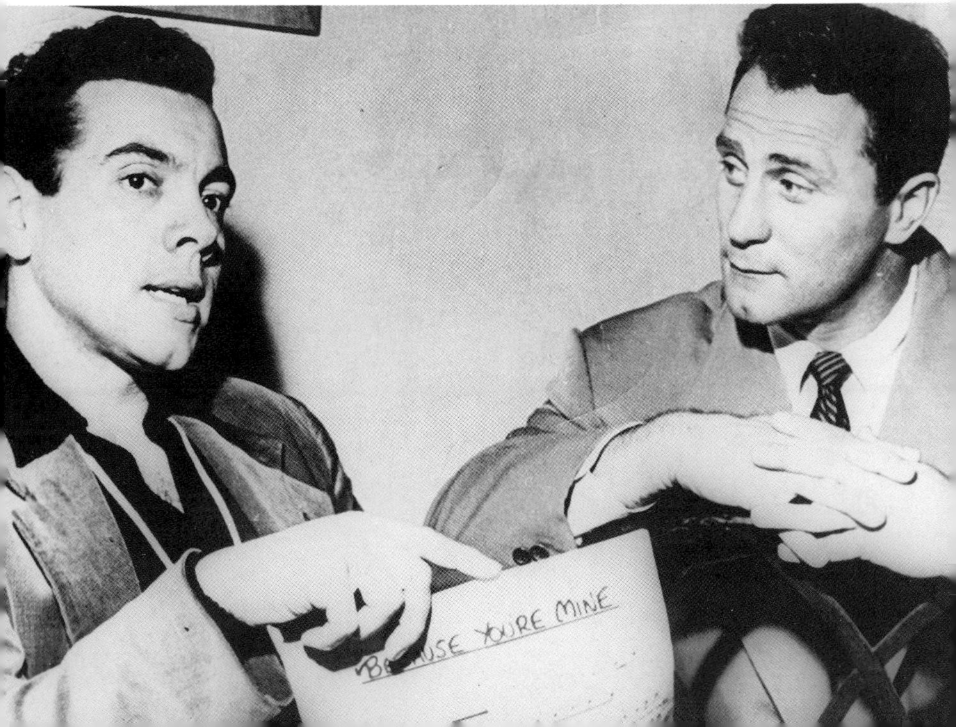

Shaking hands with Queen Elizabeth after the Royal Variety
Performance, 18 November 1957

In concert at the Royal Albert Hall with Constantine Callinicos
at the piano, London, 16 January 1958

hangers-on, it never seemed to bother him too much. Raphaela, though, was different. She first came into Mario Lanza's life when Terry Robinson happened to answer a telephone call at the singer's home from the child's mother. She had managed to obtain Lanza's number from a friend and as Terry listened to her story, a chain of events was set in motion which would, quietly and without fanfare, reach far beyond the few years that were left to both Mario Lanza and Raphaela Fasano.

For Raphaela, like Lanza, was living on borrowed time. A victim of Hodgkin's Disease, she was not expected to live long. Her greatest wish was to hear her idol sing, just once, for her alone. It was a heartbreaking story and Terry promised to do what he could. Josephine Fasano later admitted that she felt that that would be the end of it, but the following afternoon a ten-year-old child in Newark, New Jersey, received a person-to-person call from Hollywood, and an exclusive, over-the-wire recital of some of her favourite songs from the most sought-after singer in the world. Indeed, Lanza was so touched by Raphaela's plight that he arranged for the child to be flown to Los Angeles with a private nurse, where she spent five gloriously happy days at the singer's home; playing with his own children and showered with gifts and genuine affection by the man all Hollywood insisted on calling an *enfant terrible*. Thereafter, hardly a Friday evening would pass in the Fasano household without a call coming through from Raphaela's 'special friend' far away. The last call was made on 20 January 1953, when Mario Lanza was informed by the girl's father that Raphaela had passed away quietly the day before. Raphaela Fasano was laid to rest at Holy Cross Cemetery in New Jersey. Buried with her was a sterling silver Immaculate Conception Medal, a gift from the tenor.

Not surprisingly, the Fasano family never forgot Lanza's kindness, though for Josephine Fasano, that sense of gratitude went much deeper. In 1961, when the tenor's family and friends felt the need for a more permanent and lasting memorial to his talent, the Mario Lanza Foundation was formed in Philadelphia, its principal aim being the annual award of musical scholarships to promising young singers in Lanza's name. The main fund-raising event for the scholarships is a grand ball held each year in the city, usually around the time of the tenor's death. From places as far and diverse as Hungary and Ireland, fans and admirers come to Philadelphia to pay tribute and to remember. Josephine Fasano is one of those people. Hardly a year has passed since that first gathering when she has not been there, offering a quiet and dignified testament to one man's kindness and generosity of spirit.

With all the euphoria of success that surrounded Lanza in 1951 – the Caruso film, the tour, the new radio show and so on – the more astute onlooker might also have observed that that very acclaim was, in its own way, helping to turn the Great American Success Story into the Great American Tragedy. If Lanza himself had responded differently to the demands and pressures his fame had brought him, all might have been different. But given that a man is said to have the seeds of his own destruction sown within him, it was only a matter of time before something would start to go wrong.

Like many a great disaster, it all began quietly enough.

5 The Student Prince – and What Might Have Been

After the adulation and albeit grudging respect for his singing which greeted him on the release of *The Great Caruso*, Lanza was anxious to maintain that high quality of musical content in his next starring role; so when Pasternak approached him during the last days of the *Caruso* shoot with a proposal to film the Sigmund Romberg operetta *The Student Prince*, the tenor was delighted. He was already familiar with the richly melodic score, having sung a number of the songs on the Celanese radio show five years earlier. Then too, with all the lushness and expertise that MGM brought to their musicals, it seemed an ideal showcase for both the Lanza voice and frame, at the same time maintaining the quality of music now in keeping with his 'Caruso' image. Instead, through a series of delays unforeseen by Pasternak at the time, *The Student Prince* was temporarily shelved, and Lanza was compelled to start work on another project, *Because You're Mine*.

After the style and substance of the Caruso film, *Because You're Mine* marked a very definite step backwards for the tenor. The story centres on a famous opera singer who gets drafted into the army, falls in love with his sergeant's sister, and sings a lot. End of plot and start of feud between star and studio, the eventual repercussions of which were already being felt in Hollywood. From the very outset, Lanza let it be known how much he hated the idea of 'Caruso in the army'.

The storyline advanced little from his first two pictures, with the singer describing it to all and sundry as 'junk'.

Pasternak, on the other hand, saw it merely as a filler, something to keep Lanza busy while the *Prince* was being readied. In his book, *Easy the Hard Way*, he defended his decision to handle Lanza the way he did: 'I didn't want him set in the public consciousness as an opera star. I wanted him to be taken also as a man.'

Whether it was a genuine desire on MGM's part to cultivate a varied and colourful film career for their top singing star, or merely an excuse to make more millions at the box office, the studio stood firm and plans to shoot the picture went ahead. By this time too, Dore Schary had replaced Mayer as head of the studio, and it was obvious from the outset that little love was lost between him and Lanza. To the singer, Schary represented the very worst type of authority figure: domineering, officious and interested only in furthering the financial growth of the now ailing company. Under any other circumstances, such an attitude by Schary might have been laudable, but on this occasion, Lanza was on the receiving end of the corporate decisions; decisions which the tenor felt were now jeopardizing his artistic integrity.

He rebelled, perhaps unconsciously, by retreating into food, complaining all the while that MGM, Pasternak, Schary *et al.* just didn't know how to deal with an artist. By the time filming was ready to begin, Lanza weighed in at 280 lb, and this despite Terry Robinson's best efforts to keep him under control. Filming was postponed, and the rift between star and studio grew wider. Finally, though still intensely bitter at his failure to dissuade the studio from going ahead with the project, Lanza agreed to lose the weight and *Because You're Mine* went before the cameras.

This marked the beginning of a series of severe crash diets which the star would undertake many times in the years to come, and dieting would eventually place a terrible burden on his future health and well-being. By the time Lanza stepped on to the MGM soundstage for the first day of shooting, he weighed 250 lb, his heaviest ever before the cameras. Nor was that the end of it, as the wardrobe department went into overtime in an effort to try to keep up with the tenor's ever-changing waistline.

He literally weighed 250 lb when it came time to start the picture, and then one of the strangest things that ever took place in his life that I saw occurred. He began to lose weight. In the course of that picture, he went from 250 lb to 160 – no, 159 lb on the last day of shooting, and I know this for a fact because I weighed him.[1]

Given that films are shot out of sequence, the picture opened with Lanza singing an aria from *Cavalleria Rusticana* and looking thinner than he had in *That Midnight Kiss*. Then, in later scenes which had actually been shot first, he looked huge. The troubles were further compounded by Lanza's almost instant dislike of his co-star, soprano Doretta Morrow, who had been recruited by MGM following her successful Broadway debut in *The King and I*. It was a success destined not to be repeated in Hollywood however, and her on-screen love scenes with Lanza were awkward and unconvincing. Director Alexander Hall had the unenviable task of pulling the whole thing together, and it was left to James Whitmore to garner whatever acting honours there were. Lanza's parents are seen briefly in the film requesting his autograph and the tenor also saw to it that Terry Robinson was engaged to star in and stage a fight scene in the army barracks. As always though, the *raison d'être* of such a film was to highlight the particular talents of its star, and in this regard at least, 'Because You're Mine' delivered the goods. Brodszky and Cahn were again united to produce another Lanza 'classic', the million-selling title song, while Ray Sinatra contributed his own composition, 'Lee-Ah-Loo'. After *Caruso*, the operatic selections were a little thin on the ground but the film scored heavily with a thrilling rendition of 'Granada', and a moving 'Lord's Prayer', which was included in the picture at Lanza's insistence.

It was easy to see Mario Lanza's behaviour at that point in his career as arrogant and uncompromising, but then too MGM's insistence on pursuing what was at best a mediocre vehicle must also be called into question. In any event, Lanza walked away from the production emotionally the worse for wear. His reputation in the popular press as an *enfant terrible* was now firmly established, and with reports of his over-eating and disruptive behaviour now appearing with almost regular monotony in every film magazine and periodical in the country, Lanza must have wondered where the next blow was coming from.

It came, rather surprisingly, from the prestigious and usually reliable *Time* magazine, which featured Lanza on the cover of its edition of 6 August 1951. Under the heading 'Million Dollar Voice', the copywriter, unnamed, gave vent to an astonishing attack on the singer which was clearly more suited to *Confidential*. Following a few, grudging compliments of the Lanza voice, the article quickly got down to the business at hand:

> Lanza's idea of dieting is to pile chicken legs, half pound chunks of rare steak and a mound of barbecued kidneys on his plate, devour them and then heap on a second helping. For breakfast, he holds down to a steak and four to six eggs.

Then again:

> Lanza once polished off 40 pieces of fried chicken at a sitting, and washed them down with a quart of eggnog.

The reader was also reminded that:

> Mario's literary preferences lean to body building and movie fan magazines.

By the end of the first page of a three-page article, the writer had really got into full stride:

> Lanza can gorge his ego as freely as his stomach, and the studio bosses have sometimes tried needling him to deflate his head as well as his hide.

The whole sorry essay concluded with one final jibe at the Lanza voice:

> MGM's expert sound technicians, who now do virtually no tampering with Lanza's voice, can do wonders with their electronic gadgets. And ... he can always look ahead to the

all-fracturing day when some smart producer will star Mario Lanza in *The Great Lanza*.[2]

It was an outrageous and unprovoked attack on the singer and one of the rare instances when the magazine's standard of good taste and informed reporting were found completely wanting. Twelve months earlier, Lanza might well have laughed it off, but coming on top of his current difficulties with the studio, it only added to the troubles. He became irritable and moody, impossible at times for even his family to handle. Not even the choice of *Because You're Mine* for Britain's Royal Film Performance of 1952 did much to improve his troubled state of mind. He was still angry at MGM's decision to override his objections to the project, and with preparations well under way for the filming of *The Student Prince*, the battle lines were drawn for the single greatest confrontation between star and studio that Hollywood would ever witness.

If 1951 was the most successful year in Mario Lanza's career, 1952 saw Murphy's Law applied with a vengeance. Anything that could go wrong did, although it seemed at the outset that the tenor was destined for his greatest ever triumph.

With memories of the on-set feuds beginning to recede, MGM, and Pasternak in particular, were anxious to press ahead with the project that everyone felt would find the same artistic and commercial success as *The Great Caruso*. *The Student Prince* started life as a play, *Old Heidelberg*, by Wilhelm Meyer-Foerster, but it was its subsequent transformation into a musical by Sigmund Romberg, with lyrics by Dorothy Donnelly, which ensured its lasting popularity. The story had already been filmed once, as a silent film, in 1927, with Ramon Novarro as the prince, but the studio was determined that this version would be the definitive one.

Ludwig and Levien were again brought together to fashion a screenplay, their first collaboration since the Caruso film. George Stoll also returned as musical director, although Lanza insisted on having Callinicos conduct for his own numbers. As a final bonus, Pasternak agreed to the tenor's chief songwriter, Nicholas Brodszky, contributing three new songs to the existing score. Given the outstanding quality of Romberg's music, it was a daunting task for the Hungarian composer, but with the help of lyricist Paul Francis Webster and the voice of Mario Lanza for inspiration, Brodszky delivered what many believe to be the highlights of his career as a songwriter. Two of the new songs, 'Summertime in Heidelberg' and 'Beloved', were so finely crafted as to seem part of the original score, and even today, many still believe that 'Summertime in Heidelberg' was written by Romberg. How ironic, then, that one of these new songs would act as the catalyst for all the troubles that were about to follow. The man engaged by MGM to put the actors through their paces was Curtis Bernhardt, a director who, like Norman Taurog before him, was a competent practitioner of his craft. While a Gene Kelly or Fred Astaire musical required the special talents of a Vincente Minnelli or a Stanley Donen, all a director had to do on a Mario Lanza picture was to point the camera and let the man sing; that, and bring the production in on time and under budget. The quality of the supporting stars surrounding the singer and the MGM Technicolor 'look' of all their best musicals, would do the rest.

As an additional gesture of appeasement to their star, MGM again engaged Ann Blyth, this time sporting a blonde hairstyle, with whom Lanza had worked so well on the Caruso film. It all augured well for a successful production, but if Pasternak was convinced that all the essentials were covered, Dore Schary wasn't so sure, and discreet instructions were given that he be kept informed of any trouble on the set, however trivial.

Trouble wasn't long in coming, and it was anything but trivial.

In preparation for filming, Lanza set to work 'pre-recording' the songs chosen for the picture. As always, and particularly at this point in his career, the problems of excessive weight gain had to be dealt with. He felt that his best singing weight was somewhere near 200 lb, while the studios insisted that he report for filming a good 30-40 lb lighter. It was an impossible and dangerous regimen for any singer or actor to follow, yet Lanza knew that at least part of his 'movie-star' appeal depended on his maintaining a respectable waistline. Put simply, he was expected to look like Tyrone Power and sing like Caruso, and if he was quick to protest the severity of such demands, the studio was equally quick to point out the considerable fortunes that awaited him once he achieved them. So it was, then, that at his 'ideal singing weight', Mario Lanza set to work preparing for the soundtrack recordings of *The Student Prince*.

As well as the new songs written with Brodszky, Paul Francis Webster was also engaged to re-write some of Dorothy Donnelly's lyrics from the original score. The changes, for the most part, were tastefully done. In the famous 'Serenade', for example, the lines

> Could my heart but still its beating, only you can tell it how, beloved,
> From your window give me greeting, hear my eternal vow.

were changed to:

> Could I hear this song forever, calling to my heart anew, my darling,
> On I drift along forever, lost in a dream of you.

And so on. The story of the stolid, unfeeling prince who is transformed by his love for a servant girl, Kathy, delighted Lanza and for a time, he too felt that this would be the logical successor to *The Great Caruso*.

With Callinicos at the piano, he set to work rehearsing and preparing for this romantic role.

> Mario was very enthusiastic in doing this film. He worked so diligently and carefully for three weeks before we started pre-recording for the film. I've never seen him work that diligently and he didn't touch one glass of alcohol, and he was very careful with his weight, and

naturally he had stopped smoking completely. When we got to the recording studios he did an excellent job. He wouldn't have created such a musical score if he didn't want to do the film. I never saw him so enthusiastic in his whole career ...[3]

Following the rehearsals with Costa, Lanza then went to the recording studios in August 1952 and committed the score of *The Student Prince* to disc. It was his finest hour. With Ann Blyth joining him on 'Deep in my Heart, Dear' and 'Summertime in Heidelberg', Lanza recorded all of the numbers for the film in single takes. While he had completed many one-take recordings in the past, none were of the remarkable standard set down during those late summer days in 1952. It was nothing less than sheer perfection; dramatic and romantic singing of the very highest order. Soft and tender on 'Deep in My Heart, Dear' at one moment, robust and heroic the next on 'The Drinking Song', the Lanza voice captured all the pathos and charm of the Romberg score with a freshness and vitality that was breathtaking. It was that ability to breathe new life into songs such as these, an ability also very much in evidence on his weekly radio show, that made the voice so appealing to millions of admirers the world over. A unique 'sound', coupled with an intuitive sense of knowing exactly what was right for a lyric, made him the star that he was, and they were never more in evidence than on those recordings for *The Student Prince*.

Of the three new songs written by Brodszky/Webster, the weakest musically was 'I'll Walk with God', an incidental song designed solely as a bridging number between the king's death and the prince's final return to Heidelberg, and Kathy. For once, even Webster's lyrics were found wanting:

I'll walk with God, from this day on.
His helping hand, I'll lean upon ...

In lesser hands than Lanza's it could have been a disaster, but his treatment of that song, the utter conviction and truth he brought to the rather feeble lyrics, completely transcended the obvious limitations set down by the composer. It was nothing less than the soaring triumph of a great voice becoming, for two minutes and fifty-one seconds, a prayer. On the way to the recording studio, Lanza had Terry Robinson stop at a church in Beverly Hills for a moment while he went in to pray. Afterwards, immediately following the recording, he left the studio without speaking to anyone. There was simply nothing to say.

Lanza, meanwhile, had moved his parents from Philadelphia into a magnificent home overlooking the ocean, in Pacific Palisades, and it was here that he would retreat on those occasions when career demands became too great to deal with. In April, Betty announced she was pregnant again, and with his entire family now gathered around him, even Lanza began to feel that the worst was probably behind him. The 'worst', however, was only beginning.

After a brief period of dieting and exercise, a reasonably slimmed-down star arrived at MGM for the first day of studio rehearsal. The scene chosen was the one in which the prince, in an attempt to persuade Kathy to elope with him, pours forth his feelings in the romantic ballad 'Beloved'. Musically and lyrically, it was one of the very best new songs Lanza had recorded in years. He knew it and he gave it his all …

> Beloved, with all my heart I love you,
> With every breath I pray someday you will be mine.
> Summer or Spring, Winter or Fall,
> You are my life, my love, my all …

Director Curtis Bernhardt's reaction to the performance however, caught everybody by surprise, for instead of criticizing the star's obvious limitations as an actor, he chose instead to complain about Lanza's interpretation of the song. Bernhardt saw the character of the prince as cold, and virtually devoid of emotion. More restraint, much more restraint, was required of the tenor if his interpretation was to be totally convincing. Lanza couldn't believe what he was hearing. He reacted, as Callinicos put it, 'as though he had been gored', and promptly walked off the set. Dore Schary had got the report of 'trouble on the set' far quicker than even he had anticipated. The *enfant terrible*, it seemed, was back with a vengeance.

That confrontation between Lanza and Bernhardt over 'Beloved' was the single most damaging incident on the *Student Prince* set. It helped set the pattern for a whole range of confrontations and disputes which would follow and, in its own way, helped contribute to the eventual downfall of the celluloid Caruso. Lanza, of course, gave it more than a push himself. Already smarting over the studio's reluctance to increase his salary on the picture, Bernhardt's criticism of his singing just added insult to injury. In his mind, the solution to the problem was simple. Curtis Bernhardt must go. Then, and only then, would he go back and complete the film. The full responsibility for the eventual shutdown of *The Student Prince* has always been laid at Lanza's feet, but there was, nonetheless, more than one reason why things turned out so badly.

Lanza undoubtedly was difficult to handle – at times wildly uncontrollable and almost always unpredictable – but it certainly didn't take a psychiatrist to see the origins of many of his problems. Unreasonable demands were being made of him by MGM, who wanted a movie-star physique to go with the voice. And he did make vast fortunes for the studio; fortunes which were certainly not reflected in the salary he was receiving at the time. Peter Herman Adler had drawn the comparison between tenors and highly trained animals, but it was an analogy lost on MGM. Lanza was first and foremost a singer – and a remarkably gifted one at that – and a little more understanding by the studio of the real reasons behind the tantrums might have resulted in far greater dividends for all concerned. As it was, MGM's initial reaction to the tenor's walkout was to do nothing. However ill-judged his criticism of Lanza's singing might have been, Curtis Bernhardt had done nothing to warrant his dismissal from the project and Schary, in particular, had finally had it with his temperamental star.

Weeks passed, while Lanza waited for a call which

never came. It was only when a lawsuit was threatened that the singer appeared unexpectedly at a rehearsal. But the weeks of inactivity, a period not helped by the studio's strategy of staying silent, had caused Lanza to seek his usual solace in food, and the man who confronted Joe Pasternak on the soundstage that day was as far removed as could be from the svelte image of a dashing prince.

Again the film was postponed while the tenor made a few half-hearted attempts to bring his weight under control. Finally, in a last-ditch attempt to get the project moving again, a meeting was arranged by Terry Robinson between himself and Lanza's parents, with Schary, Pasternak and Metro executives Eddie Mannix and Nick Schenk representing the studio. Between them, Terry felt that some compromise could be reached and he, in particular, fought a determined battle for his absent friend. He knew, more than anyone in that room, that Lanza needed much more from MGM than an increased salary or a different director. As simplistic as it may have sounded, Terry believed that what Mario Lanza needed most of all was to be understood by Schary and Pasternak, and all those on the studio floor and at head office. If it seemed that he was making a plea on behalf of a small boy who was having difficulty dealing with grown-ups, then fine. So be it. Lanza was a child in many respects: precocious and charming one minute, petulant and unforgiving the next. But he was special, too, and different from any entertainer MGM had ever had on its payroll. The studio had to realize that, or everyone would lose – Lanza most of all. Terry knew, too, that despite all the success and wealth his film career had brought him, Lanza was still trying to come to terms with his decision to postpone his operatic career. The longer that decision was put off, the more difficult it would become to achieve his ultimate goal.

Terry Robinson spoke of all this and, up to a point, Schary listened. But he also took the opportunity to remind Robinson and the Cocozzas that no man, no matter how successful and lucrative his career was, both to himself and the studio, could dictate to that studio and question the tough decisions it sometimes had to take. The meeting concluded with everyone determined to get Lanza back to work as quickly as possible, and, for a time, it seemed as if they had succeeded.

A house in Palm Springs was rented for the star to embark on yet another series of brutal diets and workouts. Again he saw it through and by the time he returned to Hollywood, he was a fit man. But the suppleness of body did not reflect the troubled mind that lay within. Following a meeting with Schary at which only the two men were present, a terrible row broke out and Mario Lanza walked out of the studio, never to return. It was a final rift that no one – neither Terry, nor Pasternak, nor the Cocozzas – could ever heal. On 22 August 1952 an ultimatum was given to Mario Lanza by MGM to report for work the next day. He stayed away, and, on 4 September *The Student Prince* was officially cancelled.

Later that month, a lawsuit was filed by MGM in the United States District court against Lanza. He was charged with breach of contract, for which the studio claimed almost $700,000 in damages, and a further staggering $4,500,000 in general damages for the overall loss to the company for cancelling the picture. As a final crippling blow MGM also succeeded in placing an injunction on the tenor's singing career, effectively restraining him from making recordings, appearing in concert or singing on radio; this was for the remainder of his contract with them, which still had a further fifteen months to run.

In effect, Mario Lanza was a prisoner in his own home and, it seemed to many, in his own troubled mind. His troubles multiplied when he was sued by the Internal Revenue for almost a quarter of a million dollars in unpaid taxes; a claim which in turn revealed that his personal finances were in a far more perilous state than he had realized. Lanza's extravagant lifestyle, coupled with a number of bad investments by the normally shrewd Sam Weiler, had helped whittle away the bulk of his once considerable fortune. Coming on top of the MGM lawsuit, it was the worst timing of all for the turbulent star, and his paranoia and distrust of all those around him began to increase daily.

Agent Jack Keller was one of the first to go, and Sam Weiler provided his own undoing a short time later when he was interviewed by the *Dallas News* on the reasons behind Lanza's financial difficulties. Denying that the singer was as poorly off as everyone had maintained, Weiler went on to state that he himself did not need Lanza financially, claiming that he could buy and sell him ten times over. Not surprisingly, Lanza reacted to the statement like a match to paper. While MGM were preparing its lawsuit against him, Lanza took out his own personal action against Weiler. The confrontation eventually came to a head at the Santa Monica Superior Court in August 1953, when, through his attorney Milton A. Rudin, Lanza filed suit against his former manager for mishandling his affairs; he cited, moreover, an even more bizarre reason for his non-appearance on *The Student Prince* set the previous year. According to a statement issued through Rudin, Lanza had stalled production on the film simply to shut off his income until he had found a way to drop Weiler from his payroll. By suing Sam Weiler for the sum of $225,863.37, Lanza ensured that the scandal received daily coverage in the popular press. The matter was finally settled out of court the following year, when the tenor's fortunes were again on the upswing, with Weiler walking away with a deal which gave him 5 per cent of Lanza's earnings for the remainder of his career.

Joe Pasternak, meanwhile, still entertained hopes of the singer returning to the *Student Prince* set, and it was even rumoured at the time that discreet approaches were made to lure the producer's famous discovery, Deanna Durbin, out of retirement to join Lanza on the picture. But it was not to be. Miss Durbin was not interested and Lanza by now was so far ensconced in his own sense of persecution that he was virtually unapproachable to all but a few friends and relatives. His troubled state of mind was affecting all around him, particularly Betty, who was going through a difficult pregnancy. Her own solution to the problems was to resort more and more to an addictive and ever-increasing diet of tranquillizer pills.

Nor was MGM the only party interested in suing the tenor. The 'contract' signed with Irene Williams at a Philadelphia train station over a decade before represented itself before Judge Stanley Barnes at the Superior Court in Los Angeles, when Miss Williams sought compensation for unpaid fees. By now, Lanza was in no mood to argue, and a one-off, lump sum was paid without dispute to his former teacher.

Because You're Mine had opened to glowing reviews for the Lanza voice, but even the uniformed criticism of the abysmal storyline, which bore out Lanza's original complaint to the studio, did little to raise his spirits. With the MGM action preventing Lanza from working, RCA turned instead to their vast supply of Coca Cola show recordings, and thus uncovered a source of 'new' Mario Lanza material which has not been exhausted to this day. The exceptional quality of those recordings and the high volume of sales achieved by RCA ensured a fairly substantial income for the singer during his year-long battle with the studio; it was a source of income, moreover, that MGM had not foreseen when it sought to cut off his earnings.

On 15 December 1952, Betty gave birth to her third child and the family's first boy. The child was christened Damon Anthony, because of Lanza's fondness for the writings of Damon Runyon. It was the one bright spark in an otherwise disastrous year, and Mario Lanza faced 1953 with the resolution of his feud with MGM still to come.

6   The Lost Years

The final solution to the problems surrounding *The Student Prince* came in May 1953, when the studio agreed to call off its lawsuit in return for the rights to use the Lanza recordings on the soundtrack. In addition, Lanza's contract with MGM would not be renewed.

Recalling how successfully Larry Parks had acquitted himself miming to Al Jolson's recording for *The Jolson Story* seven years earlier, Pasternak felt that the filming of *The Student Prince* could still be salvaged if the right visual replacement could be found for Lanza. That replacement came in the form, the particularly slim form, of British actor Edmund Purdom, a relative unknown, who had been discovered by MGM the previous year in Laurence Olivier's touring production of *Antony and Cleopatra*, on Broadway. If it was a less than ideal compromise, it did at least ensure that Lanza's superb singing would be highlighted in the proper fashion. It has to be said too, that Purdom acquitted himself exceptionally well in the role of the prince, and although he never did get to meet with Lanza on or off the set, he would recall in later years the unique experience of working to the recordings: 'His voice was a simply fabulous voice to act to. It was an absolutely tremendous experience. I used to have the playback on the set going absolutely flat out. It was enough to make you sweat, just listening to the voice, particularly at a very high level.'[1]

The final irony, and a bitter one at that, came with the film's eventual choice of director. With all the delays incurred by the dispute, Curtis Bernhardt, the man who had inadvertently caused the original rift between star and studio, moved on to another project and was not available to direct *The Student Prince* when it finally came time to shoot. That task was given to Richard Thorpe, who had worked so well with Mario Lanza on *The Great Caruso*, and one can only wonder if the irony of that eventual choice occurred to Dore Schary or Joe Pasternak.

The Student Prince was completed in due course under Thorpe and released to moderate box-office returns in 1954, a fact which Lanza always maintained vindicated his belief that the public would never accept his singing voice lip-synched to another actor. He never saw the film, and the subject of *The Prince* was something not to be broached with him to the day he died. With his contract at MGM now expired, Mario Lanza was once again free to accept work, wherever and whenever he chose. Given the unsavoury publicity that surrounded his feud with the studio, however, other film companies were slow to capitalize on the singer's availability. Then too, the condition of the big Hollywood musical in 1953 was less than healthy, as the costs in mounting such films began to outweigh the returns at the box office.

Callinicos, in particular, felt that now was the ideal time for Lanza to turn his back on the film capital and concentrate instead on his true, and long overdue, vocation. But Lanza would not be rushed. He was still intensely bitter over the *Student Prince* débâcle, a mood exacerbated by the studio's decision to press ahead with filming without him. That period, from 1953 to 1955, marked what the conductor often referred to as the 'lost years' in the life of Mario Lanza.

He over-drank, over-ate and generally over-indulged himself to the point where Callinicos considered it an occasion when he could get him to go for a drive. The Lanza retinue now consisted mainly of Costa, Terry and the immediate family. Only a few others were allowed to penetrate his self-imposed exile, including singer John Carroll, who was having his own troubles with his studio, songwriter Andy Russell, and heavyweight boxing champion Rocky Marciano, who had been introduced to a delighted Lanza by Terry Robinson, in an attempt to lift him out of his depression. It worked for a while, too.

Lanza's love of boxing and his genuine admiration for Marciano ensured a lasting friendship between the two men. But such happy developments were few and far between. Lanza's commitment to his singing also suffered. In that entire period, he only found time to record once, in June 1953, when he and Costa were reunited at Republic Studios, almost a year after their famous sessions on *The Student Prince*. It was a one-off engagement with, as before, four songs to the booking. One of them, 'You Are My Love', had been specially written for Lanza by Costa himself; it was a pleasant, if undistinguished, number which had the benefit of a simple lyric from Paul Francis Webster. Lanza, though, was in robust voice, and the session did produce at least one classic recording. Working to Rimsky Korsakov's beautiful melody 'Song of India', lyricist Johnny Mercer wrote a superb narrative to match the music.

Then I hear the song that only India can sing,
Softer than the plumage on a black raven's wing.
High upon a minaret I stand and gaze across the desert sand
upon an old enchanted land. There's the Maharajah's caravan,
unfolding like a painted fan, how small the little race of man …

It was tailor-made for Lanza's dramatic tenor and the singer did not disappoint, completing another classic performance in one take.

It is all the more astonishing to realize, then, that over two years would pass before the voice would again be committed to disc. Part of the problem lay with the proliferation of Coca Cola songs, which RCA were now releasing at regular intervals. With such a wealth and diversity of recordings on tap, Lanza just did not bother to set up any further sessions. It was a tragic misjudgement, for it could have been an ideal time for the tenor to record complete studio performances of the great operas, but no one seems to have considered it. By the time arrangements were finally put in hand to do just that, six years later in 1959, it was too late. There was one abortive attempt at a recording in December 1953, when Lanza and Costa joined soprano Elizabeth Doubleday at the Warner Bros studio for two numbers from *The Student Prince*. RCA were putting together a soundtrack album to coincide with the release of the picture, and given that Ann Blyth was under contract to a different label, it was necessary for Lanza to re-record their two duets with another singer. In addition, Callinicos was also engaged to record the orchestral introduction to the album; but for once, Lanza's singing was found wanting.

> We began to record. His singing was faulty and bad. I couldn't begin to compare it with any of Mario's past efforts or the original soundtrack he had made for MGM. We had to put aside 'Summertime in Heidelberg' because Mario could not summon up the sweetness of quality I demanded on the number. Mario's breath control, usually fabulous, failed him. Phlegm was agitating his throat and his tones were distressingly poor.[2]

In the end, the only work salvaged from the session, aside from Costa's introduction, were two brief solos from Elizabeth Doubleday, which were eventually spliced on to the original soundtrack recordings over Ann Blyth's singing. It was the first time in Lanza's short career that his ability to perform had failed him.

With the tenor now refusing any more workouts and with his own recording work completed, Callinicos returned to New York for a number of contractual commitments. He believed that Lanza's depression, his refusal to work and his excessive over-eating and drinking, stemmed from the constant suppression of a belief that he was not fulfilling his proper destiny. However much Mario Lanza was seduced by the dream of Hollywood stardom, and all the trappings that went with it, his true, passionate, all-consuming love was for opera. His failure simply to say 'no' to the sort of life he was leading was destroying him, and if Lanza could not – or would not – see it that way, then it was up to people like Constantine Callinicos to do what they could to help. That low point in the singer's fortunes at the beginning of 1954 must have seemed like an ideal time for it, too.

At one time, in Hollywood, people accused him of being a recluse and anti-social, and so on. But he was actually soul searching, and he was trying to find ways of doing more interesting things. So we had a long talk and he said 'Costa, how about finding things for me to sing that nobody else sings ... things that are very seldom performed ... maybe do a concert with it?'
So the next time I went to New York, I visited my good friends the Broude Brothers, who have a publishing house, and I told them of Mario's desire. I looked through many scores that had not been touched for a long time and made copies of some of the things I thought would be good for Mario's voice. Well I never remember Mario being more enthusiastic ... like a little boy ... with my tiny voice I would sing them, then he'd try whatever phrases he liked in the middle and sing along with me. Every day he wanted to learn a new aria ... and that was a period of rejuvenation and discovering himself once more.[3]

The arias included works by Cilea, Mascagni and Leoncavallo; arias from long-forgotten operas like *Gloria, Zaza* and *Iris*, which deserved to be heard once more. Again though, Lanza chose to take it easy. The arias were never performed by the tenor outside that rehearsal room: a loss even more acutely felt when one considers some of the songs chosen for him to record in later years. But the rehearsals with Costa at least got him back to work, even if he was still half-hearted about performing in public. On 11 May 1954, the Lanzas' fourth and final child, a son, Marc, was born.

The pressures in the Lanzas' life were now mainly financial; so much so, that Betty was forced to send Terry Robinson with one of her most expensive furs to a man named Al Teitlebaum, a well-known Hollywood furrier, with the expressed intention of obtaining a short-term loan from the businessman. Teitlebaum, who had known the Lanzas on and off for a couple of years, was shocked to learn of the tenor's difficulties. Lanza had been without a manager since Weiler's departure, a fact which undoubtedly contributed to his current indifference to his career, and Terry felt that someone with a shrewd sense of business who knew the Hollywood set-up – someone, in fact, like Al Teitlebaum – just might be the person to get him moving again. A meeting was arranged, a deal struck, and within days, Mario Lanza found himself with a new manager, and a $60,000 advance to help clear his outstanding debts. To his credit, Teitlebaum lost no time in getting the singer back to work, although the return was not quite what everyone had planned.

Chrysler Motors, in conjunction with CBS television, were planning a new sixty-minute variety show called *Shower of Stars*, which was to go on air on 30 September 1954. It was part of a new-look image to help boost flagging car sales and the sponsors were eager to sign Lanza for the show's official launch. Television was still very much in its infancy in the mid-1950s and Lanza, like most of his contemporaries, had steered clear of it. However, with his finances in a perilous state from such a long period of inactivity, the offer from Chrysler was just too good to refuse.

For singing three songs of his own choice and appearing in a brief comic sketch with veteran actor Fred Clark, the tenor would receive a payment of $40,000, with two new Chrysler cars thrown in for good measure: a sizeable reward, particularly in those days, for what amounted to a brief night's work. The problem, when it came, was not one of content, but of presentation, for the show was to be broadcast live on the night of transmission. Very little television was pre-recorded at that time, but to Mario Lanza, unseen and unheard for over two years, the prospect of performing live in front of millions of viewers was terrifying.

What if the voice refused to perform on the night? What if the fabulous top notes didn't ring true? Remembering what had happened at the abortive re-takes of those *Student Prince* numbers nine months earlier, Lanza proceeded to magnify that initial concern until it became an obsession. The critics, he felt, were only waiting for him to fail: waiting, to prove that the greatness in the voice had finally slipped. The 'solution' to the problem, when it was found, was a remarkable misjudgement on the part of the singer and his advisors, and did more to damage his reputation as a performer in the short term than all the years of feuding with MGM put together.

For the sort of money he was being paid, the viewing public expected, and had a right to expect, a far better deal from the tenor than that which was eventually given them. For on the night of the broadcast, a hoax was played on them by CBS and by Mario Lanza; a lie, which, however well intentioned, cast serious doubts on the truthfulness and reliability of television company and performer alike.

Not that the deception was immediately noticed, however. Despite an on-screen weight of over 225 lb, Lanza seemed relaxed and good humoured, but then the main problem of the singing had already been taken care of. The numbers chosen were immediately identifiable with the tenor: 'Marechiare', 'Vesti la giubba' and 'Be My Love'. But if the man appeared in person, the voice did not, for despite some well-executed miming rehearsed over a period of several days with Callinicos, all the songs heard on the broadcast that night were recordings made two to three years earlier, in happier times. In a further attempt to disguise that fact, a slightly different version of 'Be My Love', heard only once on the Coca Cola show, was used.

It didn't work. Syndicated columnist James Bacon was one of the first to notice the deception, but when he questioned the tenor about it after the performance, Lanza denied any trickery. Matters were made worse the following day when the president of CBS in New York issued a statement saying that Mario Lanza had indeed sung 'live' on the show.

The controversy lasted for three days before CBS suddenly retracted their original statement and admitted the deception. In a cruel and sorry parallel to the saga of *The Student Prince*, Mario Lanza had now to admit to miming to his own recordings. Humiliated by his own and the television company's mishandling of the whole affair, Lanza sought to make amends. With the entire international press fully believing that the great voice had gone forever, CBS arranged for the tenor to give a special recital at his home for a select few of the city's top columnists, Hedda Hopper, Louella Parsons and James Bacon among them. With Giacomo Spadoni to accompany him on piano, Lanza proceeded to do what he should have done earlier on the Chrysler show – sing. And he sang, as Callinicos recalled, 'better than any of those reporters, columnists, soothsayers and essayists had ever heard anyone sing'. But a debt had still to be paid to his public, and given the old maxim that in showbusiness, there's no such thing as bad publicity, the Chrysler Corporation did what must have been unthinkable when the scandal first broke. They invited him back for a second appearance. Same salary, same perks. This time – 28 October 1954 – both man and voice appeared together, in what can only be described as a sensational comeback. Two numbers were chosen this time – 'E lucevan le stelle' from *Tosca* and 'Someday' from *The Vagabond King* – and it is doubtful whether Mario Lanza ever sang those songs better than he did that night.·

He was overweight, and there was no disguising the fact that he was nervous and uncomfortable, but when he stepped out from behind a curtain, raised his hands in a typical tenor's pose and began to sing, everything else was forgotten. All the pathos, all the dramatic intensity of Puccini's masterpiece, was heard in that brief performance; a performance which, when heard today, makes the despair and frustration behind Callinicos's attempts to lure him into a full-time career in grand opera, all the more acute and believable. He was, in every sense of the meaning, the popular tenor supreme and if the talent had stayed at that, if it had limited itself to the great works of Puccini and his contemporaries, then perhaps the ultimate tragedy might have been averted entirely. But it was Lanza's curse, as much as his blessing, to be able to move with consummate ease from opera to mainstream popular song, and it was this which helped trap him somewhere between those two worlds.

The second Chrysler concert, in particular, highlighted that very point. If few in the audience that night knew the first thing about opera, the sheer force and conviction of the tenor's delivery was enough to make it an exciting, thrilling experience. Then, with only a brief pause to say 'thank you' for all the letters of support since the first Chrysler show, the magic continued, though this time in a completely different mood. Lanza performed a unique balancing act which combined the power and range of Caruso with the romantic interpretation of Sinatra. Slow and sensuous the one moment, thrilling and dramatic the next, 'Someday' was beautifully done.

Whatever the purist might say about his technical shortcomings in the operatic field, in this respect at least – the effortless crossover between such diverse types of music – Mario Lanza was unique; a true original. Lanza of course, was often guilty of substituting power for sensitivity, but at his best, as that 'live' performance on television showed so clearly, there was no one to touch him. Surprisingly however, with all doubts about the quality of the Lanza voice now cast aside, the tenor once more slid into relative obscurity. He felt he had more than proved his point with the second Chrysler show and seemed disinclined to pursue any further avenues of work, at least until the $80,000 had been used up. But the Lanzas were lavish entertainers and the money wasn't long going.

His next scheduled public appearance was to be in concert at the opening of the New Frontier Hotel in Las Vegas; a two-week engagement which would net him a handsome $100,000. Lanza wasn't too thrilled at the idea of 'Caruso' singing in a gambling town, but he needed the money and eventually agreed to the booking. Ray Sinatra was signed to conduct for the tenor, their first assignment together in over three years, and with the pattern as before, an entourage consisting of Lanza, his family, servants, Terry and Sinatra, checked into a huge rented mansion in Palm Springs to prepare for the occasion.

Alternating between vocal and physical workouts, Lanza's behaviour was exemplary. By the time the party left Palm Springs in April 1955, when the city was sweltering in 100° heat, he had shed almost 50 lb in weight. He looked and sounded magnificent, and family and friends were confident of a triumphant appearance in the gambling town. Perversely though, the gambling fraternity saw it differently. That 'bad boy's' image had already preceded him and bets were already being taken, even before he hit town, that Mario Lanza would not appear on opening night. As it happened, a combination of factors banded together to ensure that the gamblers won their bets.

As always with Mario Lanza, the timing of the cancellation left everything to be desired. To begin with, Las Vegas was experiencing a freak cold spell, and coming in from the sweltering heat of Palm Springs, the inevitable happened. On the morning of the show, Lanza complained to Betty of a sore throat. Betty Lanza, herself brought to the brink of a breakdown by what she saw as her husband's increasingly neurotic behaviour, flew into a rage. The *Student Prince* disaster, the faked Chrysler show and now this. Convinced that it was just another case of stagefright, she proceeded to berate her hapless husband. Sympathy and reassurance were what he sought, ridicule and hostility were what was given him.

It is hard not to empathize with Betty Lanza on that April morning. After all the setbacks, all the costly disappointments brought on by her husband's unpredictable nature, the whole nightmare was starting again. For once though, Mario Lanza's fears were not imaginary. His throat was sore, and no matter how much critics would condemn him for forcing his voice – an accusation he always strenuously denied – nothing, no amount of money, no commitments or guarantees, would compel him to risk his voice if the production was found wanting. He stormed out of the New Frontier and headed, alone, for the Sands Hotel, and a talk with his friend, writer Ben Hecht, who was staying there. It was a form of escape, from Betty, from the concert, from commitment and responsibility, and perhaps even from himself. By the time he returned to the hotel for the evening's performance, fortified yet again by one drink too many, he was in no shape, mentally or physically, to go on.

With the venue itself now packed to capacity, the management was in an uproar. At the very last minute, when it was obvious even to Mario Lanza that he would not appear, Jimmy Durante was called in to act as a replacement. Durante did what he could to placate the furious crowd, even going so far as to claim that the singer was in an oxygen tent suffering from a respiratory infection. No one believed him, and the boos and jeers that greeted the announcement echoed far into the night.

The columnists, Hedda Hopper and Louella Parsons in particular, were merciless; Parsons perhaps came closest to the truth when she wrote: 'He suffers from the overwhelming, clutching terror that he may get up to sing and nothing will come out.'[4] The final indignity came when the Lanza family were ordered to leave the New Frontier Hotel by the management, a few days after the disastrous opening. When the family were about to board a train for Los Angeles, Lanza was asked by a reporter why he had cancelled the performance. Shaking his head with regret, he merely pointed to his throat.

But the real problem had nothing to do with the quality of the voice, which, despite everything, only continued to improve. The problem was with Mario Lanza himself. In a mind tortured by self-doubts and insecurities, he had been made a prisoner by the very thing that had brought him fame. In a rare moment of introspection and self-assessment, he had once confided to Terry Robinson: 'God gave me a voice. It's in this throat. I'm its keeper, so I have to protect it. With you – you have a voice. With me – well, the voice has me.'[5] And the voice, or the responsibility to that voice, was now slowly destroying him.

7 New Beginnings

The turnaround in Mario Lanza's fortunes came with another movie, *Serenade*, based on the book by James M. Cain and filmed by Warner Bros. Actor Edmond O'Brien had suggested the original novel to company chief Jack Warner several years earlier as having an ideal starring role for Lanza. Now, with Lanza's contractual obligations to MGM at an end, Warner finally acted on it, hiring writers Ivan Goff and Ben Roberts to fashion a suitable screenplay from Cain's sparse and steamy original. That the finished product bore little resemblance to the book was hardly surprising. It was obvious from the outset that the sole purpose of *Serenade* was to highlight the maturing Lanza voice in as many musical numbers as possible, with the storyline, as ever, taking second place to the singing. Lanza's salary was an impressive $150,000, with the added incentive of a 35 per cent bonus of the picture's gross profit. In addition, he would have the final say over the choice of music used in the film, a decision which prompted Lanza to include some of the lesser known arias, such as Giordano's beautiful 'Amor ti vieta' and Strauss's demanding 'Di rigori armato'. Excerpts such as these, the tenor felt, would help show off his vocal skills to the maximum effect, and Giacomo Spadoni was brought back once again as his vocal coach.

Warner's top musical director Ray Heindorf was put in charge of conducting, and this was the first time in his career that Lanza had recorded in a studio with someone other than Callinicos or Sinatra. Heindorf, an Academy Award winner in 1942 for his scoring of the James Cagney classic, *Yankee Doodle Dandy*, was terrifically impressed with the tenor's natural gifts. Like so many before him, he had often speculated on whether the voice was manufactured in part by some astute sound engineer at MGM. Those questions were quickly answered when the two began to record, Lanza as ever completing his chores in almost half the time allocated. The scope and range of arias in *Serenade* were by far the most demanding and complex yet attempted by the tenor in any of his films. Perhaps too much so, for the film has a heavier look and sound to it than any of his other pictures. The voice itself was richer and purer, the famous high 'C' more assured than ever. But it seemed too, as if all the doubts raised in the intervening years about the quality of that voice had somehow compelled him to substitute an over-abundance of 'fortissimo' for a sweeter, more balanced approach.

With one or two exceptions – Schubert's 'Ave Maria' or an alternate take of the film's title song, for example – the general tone of the singing was unrelentingly loud. Then too, some of the one-take numbers, such as 'Nessun dorma' or the version of the title song which closes the film, would clearly have benefited from a more studied, careful approach. Still, the voice production in general was superb, heard to its absolute best in numbers such as Cilea's moving 'Lamento di Federico' and a truly magnificent duet 'Dio ti giocondi', which Lanza sings with Licia Albenese.

In all, Albenese spent eighteen days in Hollywood working on *Serenade* and her subsequent praise of the tenor was generous in the extreme.

> You know, it really was a big voice. And I know, because I sang with so many tenors, and I can tell. But the quality, as you hear on records, was like Caruso's. So golden, so effortless. He absolutely never had any vocal problems on the recordings I heard him do. He had an infallible instinct for what was good for his voice. I don't think he studied very much. There was no need to. Coaching, yes, but not vocal studies. Everything was so easy for him.[1]

Lanza's friendship with Albenese extended far beyond the filming of *Serenade* and he always hoped one day to sing the Otello role with her on stage; a wish sadly destined to remain unfulfilled. Their duet together, and an aria, 'Nium mi tema', which he sang in his last film, do give a fascinating insight into his potential in the role: that baritonal lower register brought into full effect for the part, balanced at the same time by a beautifully controlled top 'C' of outstanding purity and power. The loss to the world of opera of such a talent was, Albenese felt, quite incalculable.

In the addition to the arias and one or two Neapolitan songs, Brodszky and Cahn were reunited one more time for two new songs for the picture: the title song, which the tenor presented in two different versions, and 'My Destiny', which became a personal favourite of Lanza's. For his co-stars in the film, Warners signed Joan Fontaine, Vincent Price, who stole the film from everyone, and a newly established actress, Sarita Montiel. Lanza saw to it that a struggling young actor friend, Vince Edwards, also got a part in the production. Edwards later went on to some fame as television's Dr Ben Casey.

The man chosen by Jack Warner to direct the picture, and who also happened to be married to Miss Montiel, was Anthony Mann, fresh from his recent success directing James Stewart in *The Glen Miller Story*. Mann had developed quite a reputation as an extremely able action director, having worked with Stewart on a number of classic westerns, *Winchester 73* and *The Man from Laramie* among them. He seemed the ideal choice but strangely enough, while the two men got on famously during the entire shoot, *Serenade* is probably Lanza's most uncomfortable on-screen performance.

He appears stiff and awkward at meeting the demands made on him by the script; the story is a rather dour affair which only manages to brighten up when Vincent Price's character appears. Then again, at over two hours' running time, it was also the longest film Lanza had appeared in, and even at that, heavy cutting was very much in evidence. Two arias found themselves on the cutting-room floor, and the lead-up to the Lanza character's infatuation with Joan Fontaine was heavily truncated, making his sudden inability to concentrate on his vocal studies because of her behaviour appear faintly ludicrous.

The filming of *Serenade* alternated between Warner Brothers' Burbank studio in California, and location shooting in the small town of San Miguel de Allende, two hundred miles north of Mexico City. Lanza's behaviour throughout the filming was above reproach. As on *Because You're Mine*, his weight fluctuated drastically during the shoot, although this time, the changes were more noticeable – as *Time* magazine, in particular, delighted in pointing out:

> He looks like a collosal ravioli set on toothpicks and his face, aflame with rich living, has the appearance of a gigantic red pepper.

The magazine, it seemed, was definitely not kindly disposed towards Mario Lanza:

> In his acting too, the tenor seems desperately afraid he will not be noticed. His eyes flash, his lips twitch, his nostrils flare, and great shudders run through his body as he mutters hoarsely to a fellow he has just met, 'How do you do?'

What even *Time* could not overlook, though, was the natural beauty of the voice:

> The big voice is just as big as ever. Lanza can still rattle a teacup at 20 paces with his 'C' and with this picture he seems sure to rattle the cash registers all across the land.[2]

Newsweek, less sarcastic overall, concurred:

> *Serenade* serves, if nothing else, to show that Lanza is still in possession of that God-given high 'C'. Summing up: Sugared Cain, fine Lanza.[3]

The most generous praise came from *Variety*, which noted:

> After three years away from pictures, Mario Lanza returns in better voice than ever. Many will find Schubert's 'Ave Maria' a tremendously moving experience as Lanza sings it in an old San Felipe church to the accompaniment of an organ.[4]

Serenade, then, was very much a return to good form for Mario Lanza and he finished the picture more relaxed and confident than he had been for years. The film premièred at Radio City Music Hall in August 1956 and was a moderate, if unspectacular, success.

The year that saw the release of *Serenade*, 1956, also marked Lanza's full-time return to the recording studios, albeit with varying degrees of success. Having broken the Callinicos/Sinatra pattern of recording by working with Heindorf the previous year, conducting honours on this session, in May 1956, fell to Irving Aaronson. Surprisingly, it was anything but a happy affair, Lanza's voice sounding coarse and thin.

The sessions took place over three days at the Warner Brothers' studios in Burbank, and consisted of a fine selection of Broadway hit tunes from the likes of *Carousel*, *South Pacific* and *My Fair Lady*, the town's newest smash. These were the type of well-crafted show tunes that Lanza had featured so successfully on his radio programme four years earlier, and the sessions with Aaronson should have been an unqualified success. As it turned out, they were anything but.

For one thing, the technical quality of the actual recording left much to be desired, having that 'echo chamber' effect which marred so many recordings from the fifties. Lanza too, was reported to be drinking heavily at the time and seemed quite incapable of obtaining any sweetness in his singing. Everything was 'fortissimo', the voice for once sounding strained on the usually reliable top notes. Indeed, there was more than a hint of operatic bellowing on some of the numbers, and the loud and forced rendition of Billy Rose's 'My Romance' bore little resemblance to the tender version of that song recorded for the Coca Cola show. One of the numbers recorded towards the end of the session, 'And This is My Beloved', does have a sort of operatic grandeur to it, but the overall effect on the listener is tedious in the extreme. The collection nevertheless proved a big seller for RCA and is still available to this day, albeit under different disguise from its original title, *Lanza on Broadway*. If the tenor had to endure many accusations of coarseness and vulgarity in his singing in the years that followed, much of the criticism undoubtedly stemmed from this particular body of work.

How remarkable to discover, then, a completely different voice three months later, this time at Republic Studios under the baton of Henri René. Where the earlier session had shown the voice production to be wanting in almost every respect, the quality of Lanza's singing at Republic was outstandingly good. For his work with René, the tenor sang a selection of songs from operettas under the title, *A Cavalcade of Show Tunes*. Most of the numbers had the backing of the Jeff Alexander Choir, which included among its singers the young Marni Nixon, later to provide the off-screen singing voices for Deborah Kerr in 'The King and I' and Audrey Hepburn in 'My Fair Lady'. For Lanza, it was a return to rare form.

Tackling numbers made popular by other singers – Allan Jones's 'The Donkey Serenade', for example, or the Nelson Eddy evergreen 'Rose Marie' – the tenor brought a freshness and vitality to the performances that virtually eliminated memories of the earlier works. His ability to make the songs sound as if they had been written specially for him was very much in evidence, and that overall production with René was easily the best work he had done in a studio since the *Student Prince* recordings with Costa. Thereafter, all the remaining songs Lanza recorded in America were done under René's direction and all to that same high standard.

With all the personal demons of the past few years seemingly put to rest, Lanza was looking for new ground to conquer, so when a European film group, Titanus–Le Cloud Productions, offered him the chance to film in Italy, he was delighted. Callinicos too, ever hopeful of the career change-over to grand opera, felt that the Italian influence on his singing might well accomplish a more mature and responsible attitude to his considerable talent.

Plotwise, the film to be made there, *Seven Hills of Rome*, advanced little from Lanza's earlier films, but it was light and undemanding enough for him to get his feet wet, as it were, in the country of his forefathers. After that, he could decide where the voice would take him. On an even happier note, MGM again became involved in Lanza's career, when they agreed to co-distribute the film. As a safeguard to his still unpredictable behaviour, the tenor was to receive $50,000 at the start of the production and a balance of $100,000 on its successful completion.

On 17 May 1957, Lanza, his wife and four children stepped on board the Italian liner *Giulio Caesere*, at Pier 84, West 44th Street in New York, bound for Naples, Italy, and a new life. On the morning of his departure, RCA threw a champagne breakfast for the singer's immediate family and friends, as tearful farewells mingled with the many wishes for much success and prosperity in the new land. It was a particularly poignant farewell for Terry Robinson and Lanza's father, neither of whom would ever see him alive again. Mario Lanza's destiny awaited him in Rome, but the groundwork for that final, sad ending to a remarkable career had already been underway for some time now. Years of precipitous weight gains and losses had done irreparable damage to his system, and all that remained for him now was to play out the final, tragic acts in the short-lived saga of the American Caruso.

Mario Lanza had just over two years left to live, but unlike those lost years in Hollywood, the time left to him was filled with renewed success and some realization at last, of his true responsibility to the voice. Sadly, that realization came too late, but its beginning, at least, was full of hope.

Lanza arrived in Naples on 28 May 1957, and it was anything but a low-key affair. Several thousand people, Caruso's son among them, turned out to greet him, and if there was also a sizeable representation from the Mafia present, nobody paid much notice. Despite looking tired and overweight, Lanza was overwhelmed. He felt that it was a good omen and even took the time to visit quietly the grave of that other great tenor whose influence all those years before had led him to this land.

While his agent looked around for suitable accommodation, the Lanza entourage travelled to Rome, where a top-floor suite at the renowned Excelsior Hotel awaited them. This was the singer's base during the filming of *Seven Hills of Rome*, but before shooting could begin, it was necessary for him to pre-record the songs chosen for the picture. As if to reassure him that his ties with America were far from severed, George Stoll flew in to take charge of the tenor's numbers, while Irving Aaronson took care of the background score. That Lanza was in a happy, expansive mood at the time can clearly be gauged from the quality of the recordings which took place at the Vatican's Auditorium Angelico. The title song for the film was also, coincidentally, the very last number written by composer Victor Young before his death. Young is perhaps best known for his award-winning score for *Around the World in Eighty Days*, and if his last song was not quite in the same category as the main theme to that particular film, it was still a pleasant number and Stoll's arrangement for once steered the tenor well clear of the obligatory high 'C' finish, hitherto essential for a Mario Lanza movie song.

Indeed, the whole musical tone of *Seven Hills of Rome* is much more mellow and relaxed than in many of the tenor's previous pictures. After the heavyweight musical content of *Serenade*, the producers felt it was time to re-establish the lighter side of Lanza's singing, and the operatic excerpts were limited to just one. The highlight of the picture was undoubtedly Lanza's rendition of the hugely popular 'Arrivederci Roma', written by his co-star, Renato Rascel. The scene featuring the number was filmed at the famous Piazza Navona, and came about purely by chance. During his stay at the Excelsior, Lanza was regularly serenaded from the Via Veneto below by a young street singer named Luisa di Mio. Charmed by the child's natural warmth and strong, clear voice, he persuaded the film's director, Roy Rowland, to include her in a scene specially re-written for the picture. In the film, Lanza plays a world-famous tenor who finds himself penniless and out of work in the Eternal City following an unsuccessful gambling spree in Monte Carlo. Walking the streets in search of work, he comes upon the child singing at the beautiful Triton fountain and trying, unsuccessfully, to earn some money. Cue for a song, of course, and the resulting duet, with the child singing at the top of her lungs while the tenor croons softly, is utterly charming.

Among the tenor's other gifts was a very real talent for mimicry. On one memorable occasion, singer Ezio Pinza arrived at a recording studio to hear what appeared to be his own voice singing a Mario Lanza song; a song, moreover, he had never recorded. It was a spot-on impersonation and Pinza was delighted, always insisting that Lanza repeat the turn whenever the two met. His impersonation of Joe Pasternak's raspy accent too, was reputedly a classic, so to emphasize even further the lighter side of *Seven Hills*, Lanza was persuaded to exercise this particular talent by impersonating Perry Como, Frankie Laine, Dean Martin and Louis Armstrong in an amusing and much-praised sequence. As with *Serenade*, Lanza was on his best behaviour throughout, and the only time that the production was held up, briefly, was when he returned to Naples for an appearance at a charity concert organized by the city fathers.

Caruso's son was also there and presented Lanza with a commemorative plaque for the occasion, but the event was marred for the singer when he learned that one of the organizers was none other than the notorious Mafia don, Lucky Luciano, who was forever trying to ingratiate himself into the tenor's affairs. It was a 'link' with Lanza's Italian heritage and one he could never quite shake off: 'This insidious organization harassed Mario through his whole stay in Italy. He never knew what it wanted of him, or what he should do.'[5]

By the time the cameras had stopped rolling on *Seven Hills of Rome*, the Lanzas had moved to 56 Via Bruxelles, a magnificent villa located in the exclusive neighbourhood of Savoia, which was once the home and grounds of the Italian Royal Family. The Villa Badoglio, as it was called, was built by the dictator Mussolini for one of his generals,

Field Marshal Badoglio. For a monthly rent of $1,000, the Lanza family had the entire run of the ground floor, which consisted of fifteen rooms, most of them inlaid in marble, surrounded by an enormous terrace. It provided ample space for the Lanza contingent, which included half a dozen servants, a cat, two dogs and several canaries. The magnificent music room echoed daily to the sound of the mighty voice and it was not long before the tenor sought out his favourite accompanist. Callinicos was conducting at that time with the New York City Center Opera Company, but with Lanza now talking about a European concert tour, he begged leave of absence and joined his friend in Rome. Columbia Artists' Management had tried for years to interest Lanza in a new tour, and always to no avail. Rome, however, was already working wonders on his morale, and by October, a full itinerary for the first half of 1958 was already well underway. First though, there was the important matter of a top-of-the-bill appearance at the 1957 Royal Variety Performance, before the Queen of England and Prince Philip. The performance was scheduled for the night of 18 November, and Lanza was thrilled at the prospect; thrilled, and more than a little apprehensive. Betty's pregnancy had prevented him from attending the 1952 Royal Film Performance of *Because You're Mine*, the first time in the history of Royal Film Performances that the star of the film had failed to appear. Now was the chance to make amends, and with Judy Garland also sharing the bill, he was determined to make it a night to remember. Since the completion of *Seven Hills of Rome*, Lanza had brought his weight under control and he looked terrific, every inch the movie-star.

Just before he left for London, he agreed to be a guest on a twenty-minute film, *The Christopher Programme*, which was specially filmed at the Vatican for a Catholic charity organization based in New York. The format of the show was an interview between Lanza and the organization's founder, Father Keller, who chatted to the singer about his life and career. A new addition to the Lanza camp, Paul Baron, accompanied the tenor on piano for three songs, and as a special bonus, Betty Lanza joined him for part of the interview. Together, they presented a picture of marital bliss, and if in truth their relationship was not as idyllic as it appeared – Betty by now depending more and more on tranquillizers than was healthy – the couple nevertheless continued to rely on each other totally. Life without Mario Lanza was an unthinkable prospect for Betty Lanza and she herself would not last long after the tenor's death two years later.

Tragedy was far from everyone's thoughts however, when the Lanzas and Callinicos set sail in November 1958 for London and an engagement with the Queen of England.

8 The Final Tour

Lanza arrived by the *Golden Arrow* train at Victoria Station on 14 November and was promptly knocked off his feet by a surge of several hundred screaming fans. A news crew from London Weekend Television was on hand to capture the moment as the delighted singer was borne to safety by the police. 'Be My Love' might not be top of the hit parade any more, but the fans had clearly not forgotten Mario Lanza. For the duration of the tour, the tenor's welfare was put in the capable hands of John Coast, acting for Columbia Artists, and Peter Prichard, Leslie Grade's representative. It was Grade who organized the Palladium appearances and both parties did everything in their power to ensure a happy and trouble-free stay. But trouble, as ever with Mario Lanza, was never too far away. A press conference was called for the following day at the Dorchester Hotel where the Lanzas were staying, and it was here that the first hint of the tenor's infamous temperament began to manifest itself. Despite the fact that he was looking remarkably slim and fit, the inevitable questions about his weight were not long in surfacing. The more Lanza tried to brush aside the queries, the more persistent some of the reporters became. It was his first introduction to the questionable standards of British tabloid journalism and he wasn't prepared for it. Barely keeping his temper under control, he managed to stop short of being outwardly rude to the gathering, but it was clear that what had started out as a happy, uncomplicated affair, was quickly turning into something quite the opposite.

Fearing a repeat of the disastrous cancellation at the

New Frontier Hotel, Callinicos did his best to keep the singer calm. In his book, *The Mario Lanza Story*, the conductor insists that the tenor went on a three-day drinking spree in his hotel, refusing to attend the rehearsal for the event, and only managing to pull himself together at the very last minute to attend. The story of the cancelled rehearsal was also reiterated by Costa in a radio interview in 1974, fifteen years after Lanza's death, but in this respect at least, his memory was definitely found wanting. Lanza *did* attend the rehearsal, admittedly tense, as a series of photographs and comments from other artists participating in the show bear out. The singer's nervousness prompted him to insist on clearing the stage while he ran through his numbers – a fact which caused some misunderstanding and more than a little annoyance among several of the cast, British comedian Arthur Askey among them, who saw it only as an example of American movie-star rudeness. But rude or not, Lanza had come to sing, and it was left to the show's musical co-ordinator, Cyril Ornadel, to comment on the preparations for the performance, and the voice.

> When the rehearsals started, his conductor Constantine Callinicos came and took over the orchestra, and I sat down by the side of him [Lanza]. First of all, Callinicos ran the orchestrations through and Mario Lanza was just sitting in the stalls. When he was ready, Lanza came up on the stage and they started to run through the numbers, and we were shattered to find that every word and every bar was mouthed by his conductor, and it suddenly became apparent that Mario Lanza couldn't sing a note or a phrase or a bar, without his conductor guiding him through the sequence. But when you stopped looking at that, you just listened to this gorgeous, natural voice that was singing so beautifully.

Ornadel's assessment of Lanza's ability to sing without Costa's guidance was of course, incorrect; the claim was, moreover, refuted by the conductor when he heard about it later on. Costa's mouthing of the lyrics for Mario Lanza was a standard practice between the two men whenever the tenor was nervous or ill at ease. It had been done on the infamous first Chrysler show and was repeated now simply for reassurance. On their concert tours, with Costa providing piano accompaniment only, Lanza performed with his back to him, prompting only being given when a line was forgotten or out of place.

There were no such problems on the night of the Royal Variety Performance though, as Cyril Ornadel also recalled.

> The Command Performance was on a Monday night, and then he did a *Sunday Night at the London Palladium* on the following Sunday to widely varied audiences. On the night of the Royal Command, which is generally known as a sort of stuffy audience, he got royal acclaim. Absolute roars, which is most unusual for there. On the following week, when you again have a different sort of audience, they tore the place up.[1]

It was a total triumph, proving yet again that Lanza's occasional doubts about his ability to perform were based solely on his own deep-rooted insecurities and certainly not on any lessening of his powers as a singer. On 24 November, following his second appearance at the Palladium, the Lanzas and Callinicos returned to Rome, where plans for the tenor's new-year tour of Europe were being finalized.

In this happy frame of mind, an ambitious, 44-date concert tour was scheduled by Columbia Artists to begin in England the following January; a tour which would take Lanza and Callinicos through the British Isles, including Scotland and Northern Ireland, to France, Belgium, Holland and a number of venues in Germany.

In many ways, it was the 'Caruso' tour all over again. Within hours of its announcement, every venue on the list was completely booked out, with renewed appeals for more dates to be added to the schedule. Everyone, it seemed, wanted to hear the voice at first hand. Sadly however, it was destined to be Mario Lanza's farewell to his public, for it was on this tour that the first real warning signs of his declining health became evident.

Of the forty-four dates booked, Lanza managed to

complete only twenty-three. The tour started out well enough, with the tenor in top form for a concert in Sheffield, England, on 4 January 1958.

> The fabulous star of MGM musicals opened his British concert tour at City Hall, Sheffield to a capacity audience of nearly 3,000. Four weeks ago, when booking commenced, every one of the seats was snapped up in the record-breaking time of two hours.
>
> ...the magnificent 'Stars Were Brightly Shining' from *Tosca* produced an ovation he is not likely to forget ... and the finale, 'La donna e mobile' was a great thrill.[2]

Appearances at Glasgow, Newcastle and Leicester followed, and on 15 January Lanza returned to London to greet Betty, who had flown in from Rome in preparation for her husband's debut at the Royal Albert Hall the following evening. It promised to be a memorable occasion all round, with Lanza performing to a capacity audience of over 7,000 and RCA Victor recording the event for posterity. In a happy and expansive mood, the Lanzas spent the night before the concert at the opera. American tenor Richard Tucker was set to make his debut at Covent Garden in a new production of *Tosca*, and Lanza asked if he and Betty could attend the performance. Tucker was delighted, and saw to it that they sat with his wife Sara, in the singer's private box.

> Lanza, not wanting to call attention away from Tucker and the stage, insisted that he sit in the rear of the box, out of the public's view. Sara understood and appreciated the gesture, knowing well of Lanza's celebrity – a fact underscored by the eight thousand screaming fans who packed the Royal Albert Hall for each of his concerts.

After the performance, the two couples returned to Lanza's suite at the Dorchester for a late-night supper and much happy talk.

> Tucker ate leisurely while Lanza drank large quantities of mineral water and German beer. Lanza ate nothing all evening, and explained that he was on a strict diet. For the

rest of the evening, the two men talked like long lost friends, about their childhoods, years of vocal training, first breaks, their religious backgrounds, ethnic roots, family lives – topics normally reserved for classmates at a reunion, and unusual for two men who had nothing more in common, ostensibly, than their American birthplaces and tenor voices. In retrospect, Sara reflected, 'It was as if Mario wanted to figure out why Richard's life had gone one direction, and his own life another. He was very subdued and seemed to hang on to every word Richard spoke. He seemed to want and need a friendly ear, and in Richard he found one. Richard and I both got the impression that for all his wealth and great success, Mario wasn't really happy. Something important, something very basic was missing from his life.[3]

Lanza's own performance at the Albert Hall the following evening also marked a double 'first' in his career: the first time he had been recorded in concert and the first time the voice had been captured in stereophonic sound. On all fronts it was an outstanding success. The singer was in superb voice on the night, and despite being visibly startled by the size of the hall when he stepped out on to the stage – 'Is this real?' he asked the delighted crowd – the performance that evening was one of his very best. Starting with some of the programme's heavier numbers, such as 'Lasciatemi morire', Lanza took his time winning over the audience. By the sixth song, however, 'Bonjour ma belle' – 'a very, very sexy song about a passionate Englishman and a French girl' – they were eating out of his hand. The wave of applause that greeted his final number on the programme was deafening, surprising even Lanza, who felt he had heard it all by now. 'Wow, thank YOU!' he responded, before encoring with the inevitable 'Because You're Mine'.

It was the only time on the European tour that he sang at the same venue as his idol, Enrico Caruso, had done. Caruso's own debut at the great hall in 1908 had been marred by the news that day of his father's death, and the added despair of hearing that his common-law wife had eloped with his chauffeur. For Lanza there was no such tragedy, and Betty's presence in the hall that night made the triumph all the sweeter.

On 22 January, Lanza and Callinicos left London by air for Germany, and a further tour which would take them to Munich, Stuttgart, Hamburg and Baden-Baden. It was here that Callinicos first began to notice a disturbing change in the singer's health.

At the end of the Munich concert, the enthusiastic Germans converged on the stage, making it almost impossible for us to get off. At one time, this kind of response from his fans would have delighted Mario. Now it was unnerving, upsetting. Afraid the audience might react the same way at Stuttgart, Mario asked me to make an announcement before the concert that he would gladly sing encores if they promised not to rush the stage at the end. I made the announcement. But the spectators broke their word, and moved on Mario. By the time we escaped, Mario was exhausted. It wasn't like him. Something was wrong.[4]

A doctor was summoned to his hotel the following day and diagnosed high blood pressure and phlebitis in his right leg. Immediate rest was ordered and the two remaining concerts in Hamburg and Baden-Baden were reluctantly called off. Only three weeks into the tour, the cancellations had already begun, although this time it had nothing to do with the whims and vagaries of a temperamental star. The years of over-indulgence and rich living, and the mad, brutal rounds of abstinence and crash dieting that followed, were finally beginning to catch up with Mario Lanza. Back in Italy, his leg badly inflamed, the tenor was hospitalized briefly, and a further seven appearances scheduled for Great Britain the following month were cancelled. John Coast had accompanied Lanza on the first part of the tour and was distraught by what he saw. On his return to London, he immediately dispatched a lengthy and heartfelt plea to the singer which had in it a disturbing portent of the tragedy still to come.

Mario, my friend, this is a very serious letter to you, written just as much from me as a human being as from a concert agent. First, let me say this. From the start I have had the very highest opinion of your voice. But when listening to you in that fantastic concert in Stuttgart the other night, I felt absolutely confident and sure that yours is the greatest living Italian tenor, and also the only truly robusto one ... your voice was not only black and warm and dead on pitch, but it was strong as a pillar from top to bottom – it showed no trace of thinning at the top or in any other register – and purely as a lover of a good voice I said to myself: 'This man must *not* be allowed to destroy himself; this man *must* do the many things in his career which he still can do and should do.' I tell you – Di Stefano, Del Monaco, even Jussi – they're not in the same league with you at all. And this brings me to my second point, which is your health. Mario, that doctor in Munich is a hell of a good man. I trust him and his opinion because his medical opinion agrees with my common-sense-deduction. He told you last night what he told me a day before – that you might easily kill yourself within a year if you couldn't get your physical and personal problems straightened out. He said that one day you might have some sort of a clot and just pass out.[5]

Coast shared his concern with Bill Judd of Columbia Artists back in New York, who also took the time to write to the tenor at the Villa Badoglio, but Lanza shrugged the gloomy predictions off and ignored the letters. He resumed the tour on 3 March, his bandaged leg resting on a chair at the Dorchester for all the world – courtesy of the camera press – to see. Five more concerts were completed as scheduled, but it was obvious to all around him that he was in great distress. On 15 March, he returned again to Rome, this time for the confirmation of his daughters, Colleen and Ellisa. Five more concerts were cancelled as a result of his health, and by now it had become a matter of speculation as to where and when he would next appear. A recital in Dundee, Scotland, on 27 March was honoured, but was followed by a cancellation at City Hall, in Newcastle, and so on. Callinicos found it particularly ironic that at a time when Lanza actually had a valid excuse for the cancellations, many of the popular papers continued to insist that it was just another example of Mario Lanza's arrogant and fickle attitude toward his public. Even the tenor's constant use of a walking stick to support his inflamed leg was seen as little more than a cheap publicity stunt; a facile attempt to appease promoters and public alike. Those who did manage to see him however, continued to be enthralled.

At the King's Hall in Belfast, on 29 March, a capacity audience of over 8,000 screaming fans showed their approval, but his next stop on the tour, at the Paris Olympia, unexpectedly found him in poor spirits. There was nothing wrong with the voice, but the lack of stamina was starting to show. Two concerts in Belgium and Holland followed, and the tour concluded in Germany, where, scheduled to give three performances, Lanza was on hand for only two. Hanover was the first stop, where an echo of the old days in Shippensburg, Ohio, suddenly re-presented itself to a less than impressed music critic of the *Hanoverische Algemein* newspaper.

> It began when a man walked on to the stage of the Niedersachshalle. It was not Mario Lanza, the world famous tenor, but one of his managers, who apologized for the fact that Lanza's evening dress had not arrived because of unforeseen difficulties and would the public forgive him. Then a stockily built, broad shouldered Italianate man walked forward to acknowledge the applause of the welcoming audience. His appearance was pure American slovenliness – a lounge suit and a crooked tie, and later, he drank water in full view of his public. The whole scene reflected the circles in which the star moved, a pre-packed bundle of 'public relations' sent to Europe at just the right time, filling the gap after Gigli ...

But if the on-stage manner and appearance left something to be desired, the voice more than compensated:

> Ever since Mario Lanza starred in *The Great Caruso*, his name has been known throughout the world. And rightly so, for there is no equal to this naturally beautiful tenor voice in the world today. The free-flowing 'bel canto' is an

irresistible attraction, the unsurpassing strength flowing from the heights of falsetto to a deep, coaxing urgency ... nothing could deprive the evening of the infatuating attraction of the voice. Indeed, the enthusiastic reception knew no bounds.[6]

Two nights later, on 13 April 1958, Lanza appeared at the vast Österhalle, in Kiel, and it was here that the great voice was heard in public for the last time. Despite the fact that the tenor was fighting a cold, for Costa in particular it was an unforgettable farewell. 'He seemed that night ... at the mammoth indoor stadium in Kiel, Germany, to be at the height of his powers as a singer. His voice, "darker" and richer than I had heard in years, thrilled me. Its volume and substance rivalled any male voice I had ever heard in my life.'[7] It was an opinion echoed the following day by music critic Dr Kurt Klukist, writing for the *Lubecher Nachricten.*

The hall was still. It had begun. Italian arias, folk songs, Puccini, English 'pop'. One thing was obvious after the first few bars ... this man, who was not allowed to be other than the product of a well-regulated publicity machine, fell naturally and significantly into the greatest role he could play ... he really can sing. The material belonging to this wonderfully melodious tenor is a natural gift. Lanza has a 'strad' in his throat and he understands how to use it. It is difficult to know what to admire the most. The faultless breathing technique, the elastic precision of his wording. The light 'piano'. The constantly disciplined 'forte'. The well-synchronized join between registers. Lanza sings emotionally, a smouldering fluency. His delivery is definitely not a technical exercise but an event of blessed southern sensuality. Characteristic of the Italian style of singing are the famous 'tears' in the voice, that small pretence learned from the sobbing of the nightingale that most Italian tenors put on, but here is a completely natural sound. When he is not singing, he seems a little nervous, perhaps the aftermath of a serious illness. When he sings, he is fully relaxed. He pulls his tie undone, opens his collar because of the heat. Applause, and more applause. An encore is dragged out of him – or is it two? Then, with a gesture of typical romantic panache, he says goodbye ...[8]

Eight scheduled appearances remained to complete the tour, including a thirty-minute concert for BBC Television from the Brussels World Fair, set for 28 April. All were cancelled following a disastrous non-appearance at Hamburg on 16 April. Having already missed out on one performance in the city at the beginning of the year, no one expected any difficulties once the venue had been re-booked. Lanza and Costa arrived a day early, but the cold which had been bothering the tenor in Kiel had worsened. On the day of the performance, his throat was visibly raw. One doctor was called, then two, and by the time Callinicos arrived dressed for the engagement, he was told bluntly that the singer was in no condition to perform that evening. In a sense, it was Las Vegas all over again, for by now the hall was filling up with thousands of people keenly anticipating the big event – including Herr Collien, the concert manager, still blissfully unaware of the singer's indisposition. The concert, set for 8.15p.m., was cancelled at 7.55. Callinicos travelled to the hall to try to explain the cause of Lanza's trouble but by then the crowd were in no mood to forgive.

> The moment Herr Collien got my name out of his mouth, the crowd went wild with its derisive shrieking and howling. During the 'Caruso' tour I thought I had seen everything in the way of unruly, obnoxious behaviour, but I had to go to Hamburg to see my first concert hall 'lynch mob'. They came at me, pressing up to the stage, milling around me, shoving and stamping. Photographers had climbed on top of the grand piano and were snapping away at me. An elbow caught me in the ribs. For a long time I stood there, transfixed by the ferment and uproar. Then, my heart palpitating, my hands trembling, I worked my way backstage. With a police escort, I was at last on my way out of the hall.[9]

The nightmare continued for a time at the hotel, with police posted at the front and rear to prevent a small crowd of incensed ticket-holders from taking their grievances out on the ailing tenor. It was a vicious, ugly, thoughtless reaction to the cancellation, and it left Callinicos in particular, shaken and distressed. To Lanza though, the audience reaction was one of disappointment; regret that they hadn't heard him sing. In his mind, the solution was a simple one. He would return to Hamburg soon and give them all a performance they would never forget. All the transgressions would be forgiven, and Callinicos, the ever reliable Costa, would be there to share in the glory of it all. It would be soon, just like the postponed operatic performances that were always being promised for next month, or next year. But Mario Lanza was thirty-seven years old, and those 'next years' were finally down to one.

9   For the Last Time

By April 1958, Lanza was back in Rome, his beleaguered management team trying to cope with the offers of work which were still coming in. Despite the Hamburg fiasco, or perhaps even because of it, everyone it seemed, still wanted to hear Mario Lanza sing. From venues as far away as South Africa, New Zealand and Australia, and with guarantees running as high as $10,000 for a single appearance, Lanza was tempted. The offer from South Africa was particularly attractive and for a time, the tenor even considered going.

But with his health and his mood changing almost daily, even Callinicos, who was staying at the Villa Badoglio, began to question the viability of the trip. In his heart, Lanza knew he was wasting his considerable talent. If he had hoped, in Rome, to escape the constant urgings and pleas of friends and colleagues alike to give up the movie world and concentrate on the stage, he was sadly disappointed. If anything, Rome had made matters worse, acting instead as a constant rebuke of his careless attitude towards a blessed gift. All around him were constant reminders of his true and all-consuming passion.

Di Stefano, then at the height of his considerable powers as a singer, was a neighbour and constant visitor to the Villa Badoglio. And Callas was achieving the sort of mass adulation at the opera house that many felt Lanza would have enjoyed too. What a pair they would have made. But it was Lanza's lack of high purpose, and that alone, which kept him where he was, and by April 1958, the strains caused by that irresponsible stance were at last beginning to take hold. Some idea of the tenor's troubled state of mind can be gleaned from an excerpt from a diary kept by Lucie Miller, a maid at the Villa Badoglio at that time.

Now, what Callinicos and the rest of the household fear the most, has happened. The authorization for his South African tour has come through. He is to receive $10,000 a concert. It arrived the day before yesterday. Lanza hasn't seen it yet. He refuses to sign anything. He sits in the basement kitchen and drinks vast quantities of beer, almost as though he wanted to be too ill to go. He certainly couldn't travel in his present state, let alone sing. This is only my first month at the Villa Badoglio but I know already that this is not the first time he has sought refuge with the kitchen staff. He sits looking out of the window reaching for one bottle after another. This is the first time I have seen him at such odds with himself and the world. I can't help feeling deeply sorry for him. It's no secret that this young man from Philadelphia is more at ease with ordinary people. He has left behind their environment but he can't leave behind their way of life. All the porters at Rome station know that they can go up to him and ask him 'How are you, Mario?' Every hotel porter and vegetable seller knows that he'll not only give them money, but he'll sing for them too. I met him today on the way to the kitchen. He looked at me out of his swollen, doleful eyes ... 'I can see what you're thinking,' he complained. 'You think what those doctors think, what they all think. He'll die soon ... Caruso died young. But I won't die ... I won't die. I don't want this stuff anymore ...' Then he wandered away, glassy eyed, into the kitchen.[1]

Lanza's sense of the dramatic inevitably led him to make comments about premonitions of an early death, and the family had come to ignore them. It was his way of feeling sorry for himself and was usually brought on by exhaustion after a gruelling tour or film schedule. By 1958 though, his health had genuinely deteriorated and not surprisingly, the South African tour fell through.

With little for him to do, Callinicos considered returning to America and the New York City Opera, but his departure was delayed when word of yet another picture for Lanza surfaced in Rome. If the conductor had questioned the singer's ability in the past to surmount his own private demons, he knew more than ever now, that the sheer effort needed to conquer his present difficulties would take all the reserves of will-power that Lanza had within him. Amazingly, he was able to do it. The drinking stopped, the eating was brought under control, and the daily despair became, for a time, a thing of the past.

Preparations for work on what was to be the tenor's final film, called, ironically, *For the First Time*, began in the spring of 1958. The storyline again left much to be desired. A temperamental tenor falls in love with a beautiful deaf girl and determines that one day she will hear him sing. Visits are planned to the top ear specialists throughout Europe, a successful operation is performed, and the girl awakens to the sound of her beloved softly intoning Schubert's 'Ave Maria'. It was a long way indeed, from the quality scripts the tenor had been demanding after *The Great Caruso*. But despite the storyline, *For the First Time* proved to be Mario Lanza's most accessible film in years. It was produced by Alexander Gruter for Corona Films in West Germany, and MGM again agreed to co-produce. On 5 May 1958, Lanza signed a contract guaranteeing him $200,000 plus a percentage of the profits. As usual, the weight had to be brought under control and the film company's insurers arranged for the tenor to undergo a preliminary examination with a Doctor Fruhwein, in Munich, where part of the picture would be filmed.

The prognosis was alarming. Over-acidity in the urine was discovered which was causing gout, there were signs of disorder in the heart and liver, both of which were of abnormal size, and his blood pressure was distressingly high. The doctor also found signs of hardening of the arteries and the general, depressing diagnosis was sufficient for the tenor to be dispatched to the Park Sanatorium, in Walchensee, Bavaria, for complete rest and treatment.

Walchensee had become famous for its 'twilight sleep' treatment, by which patients were fed intravenously to help them lose weight, and it was to this particular practice that the singer surrendered his tired and ailing body. For a man in Lanza's condition, it was plainly courting disaster, but the producers were waiting and the weight had to go. He was a difficult patient, quickly becoming bored and resentful at the spartan dieting and light exercises, and when Callinicos visited him in June, Lanza took it as an opportunity to visit the nearby resort town for a few furtive beers. He was as incorrigible as ever, but Costa knew by now that the time for change was gone for ever.

Remarkably though, as the man went to ruin, the voice grew even more prodigious. The true quality of that voice was put to the ultimate test in late August 1958, when Lanza and Callinicos returned to Rome to record the operatic selections for the film. The producers had arranged for the recordings to take place at the Rome Opera House, with the company providing the orchestra, soloist and chorus members as back-up. It was Lanza's toughest audience since the days of the *Caruso* recordings with Adler and soloists from the Met, and even those sessions had taken place on an MGM soundstage, a far cry from the openness of the opera stage. This time he was right in the firing line. No mercy would be shown if he got it wrong. Callinicos was in no doubt about the quality of the voice, only its ability to respond to this new challenge.

We started working. None of the orchestra members or anybody else working at the opera house had ever heard Mario sing 'live'. Now they hear him on the stage of the Rome Opera House and they are absolutely charmed. They all thought that Mario's voice was the kind that needed all sorts of electronic equipment to magnify it. So after each number I was getting the reaction of the musicians who were sitting close to me at the podium and it was all in the sense of 'Maestro, we never knew that Mario could sing? We never thought that he has a voice like this?' One of these remarks came from General Director [Ricardo] Vitale who said ... 'I never knew how Mr Lanza sounded in person and I would like to ask you now to be a go-between and see if he would be interested in singing Cavaradossi in *Tosca* during our opening of the Rome Opera season.' He thought Mario's voice was being magnified by electronic equipment. He never knew it was such a glorious voice.[2]

But if Callinicos was delighted at such an offer, Lanza – although pleased at the compliments which greeted his performance that day – still remained uninterested in pursuing his career along those lines.

With film and recording commitments now looming, he turned down the offer for the time being, although Costa would later insist, shortly before Lanza's death, that agreement was reached with Vitale for the singer to open in *Tosca* at the 1960 season. That he had all the powers necessary to have made it an unforgettable occasion there can be no doubt, but given Lanza's very real problems with self-discipline and his unpredictable nature, the possibility of that performance ever taking place, even had he lived, must be open to question. As a result of the recording session that day, word of mouth quickly spread from Vitale and the musicians, and offers from many of the great houses throughout Europe and South America began to come in. He could have his choice of role, his choice of partner, and so on. Lanza though, just didn't want to know, and it was left to Callinicos to deal with the requests as tactfully as he could.

In addition to the operatic numbers with Costa, Lanza also recorded selections with Carlo Savina and George Stoll, including a new number specially written for him by that conductor, 'Pineapple Pickers', which has the distinction of probably being the worst song ever recorded by Mario Lanza. It was a horrible, pseudo-rock and roll effort which even managed to obliterate memories of the infamous 'Boom Biddy Boom Boom' eight years earlier.

Still, after the over-abundance of grand opera in *Serenade* and the almost complete lack of it in *Seven Hills of Rome*, *For the First Time* did manage to get the balance right for a change – 'Pineapple Pickers' notwithstanding. The film was shot on location in Capri, Paris and Germany, and was lovely to look at, a fact which undoubtedly owed much to its director, Rudolph Maté. Maté's reputation rested on his years as a distinguished cinematographer, when he worked on such classics as Dreyer's *Vampyr*, Hitchcock's *Foreign Correspondent* and Lubitsch's *To Be Or Not To Be*. His mid-career changeover to director was less successful – the minor *noir* classic *D.O.A.* probably being the best of a fair lot – but he knew what was expected of him on a Mario Lanza musical and he did his job well.

The staging of the operatic scenes in particular was superb, and when Lanza, in full Radames regalia, turns his back on the audience at the conclusion of the *Aïda* grand march which closes the film, it is a fitting and somehow poignant farewell. Hanging over the film, too, was the tenor's own premonition of an early death, as one of his co-stars in the picture, Hans Sohnker, recalled.

On 15 November, we were invited to a cycle race at the Berliner Sportsplatz. I joined him there just after he had learned of the death of his actor friend, Tyrone Power. Power was forty-five years old and had died of a heart attack while making the film *Solomon and Sheba*. Lanza was quite distracted. He wrote a letter of condolence immediately. A visitor walked in later and asked for his autograph. He took out his pen and blotted the ink on a serviette. With an abstracted despair, heightened by several glasses of wine, he murmured, 'I won't die ... I won't die like Tyrone ...' Then he drank more.[3]

That the Lanza temperament had mellowed over the years was very apparent during the filming of *For the First Time*, as his co-star in the picture, Zsa Zsa Gabor, soon found out.

Before I met him, I heard so many terrible things about him. That he's rude, that he uses foul language and everything. I must say I spent six months with him and his family in Rome and Capri, and in Berlin, Germany, and I thought he was the nicest, kindest man I ever met. He was a sweet, darling man. I adored him and his wife Betty ...[4]

For the First Time was completed on time and under budget, and the picture opened to excellent box-office returns on 8 August 1959, backed up by some of the best reviews the singer had had in years.

> Mario Lanza's voice is in top form in his latest film. Not only is he in splendid voice, but he ranges from Rock n' roll to love songs. For cinemagoers there is no weak spot in the musical content.[5]

> One of the better screen vehicles for Mario Lanza. His delivery of 'O sole mio', 'Vesti la giubba' and the final aria from *Otello* are splendidly rendered.[6]

> Mario Lanza sings better than ever.[7]

Lanza himself felt it was the best singing he had done on film since *The Great Caruso*, an opinion shared by RCA when they renewed his recording contract for another five years at a yearly income of $200,000. The first recording under that new contract took place in Rome, in late November 1958, when the tenor joined forces with conductor Franco Ferraro for an album of Neapolitan songs eventually released under the title *Mario*. Several of the numbers were arranged by an up-and-coming young musician by the name of Ennio Morricone, later to achieve great fame as a film composer on such epics as *The Good, the Bad and the Ugly* and *Once Upon a Time in America*. As to the selection of songs chosen for the album, Lanza sang them all to the manner born, in a voice of superb richness and power. One song in particular. 'Voce e notte', became, in his own words, 'my favourite recording' and when the master tapes from the session reached New York, RCA executives were enthralled. His old friend Richard Mohr immediately dispatched a telegram to the Villa Badoglio:

> Just a note to tell you how excited all of us are about your forthcoming album of Neapolitan songs. You and Ferraro certainly co-operated beautifully and I have seldom heard you sing better than this. I know the record will be a success, if only on the basis of something like 'Dicitencello

Royal Albert Hall concert, 16 January 1958

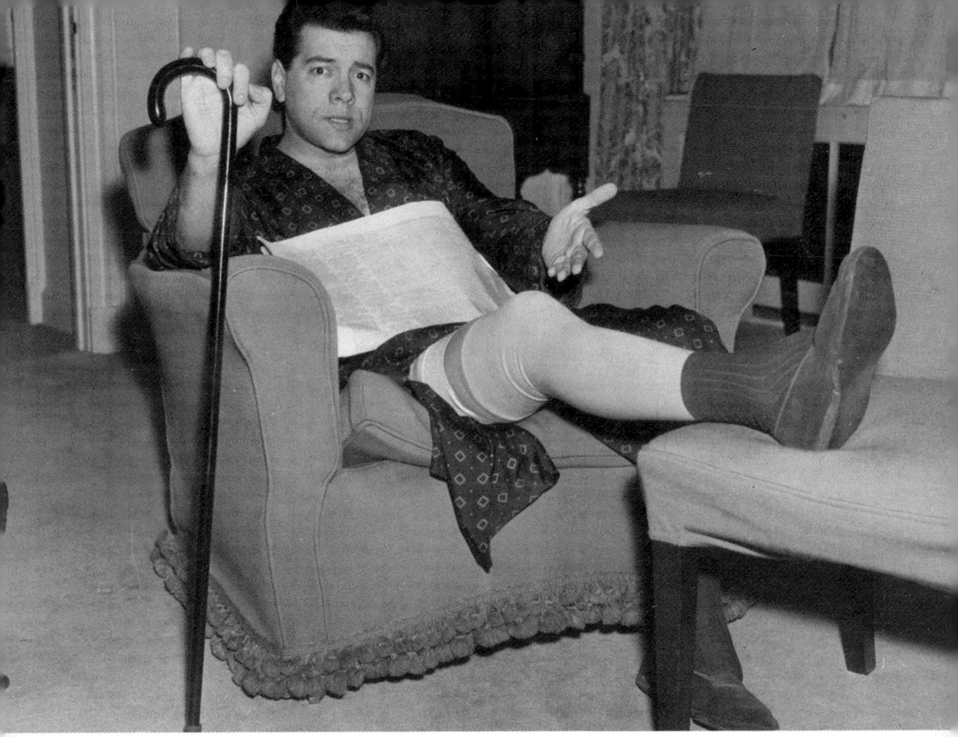

Leg in elastic bandage after a bout of ill health, Dorchester Hotel, London, 3 March 1958

Rudolph Maté directs Lanza in a scene from *For the First Time*, Salzburg, Austria, 1958

Death scene from *Otello – For the First Time*

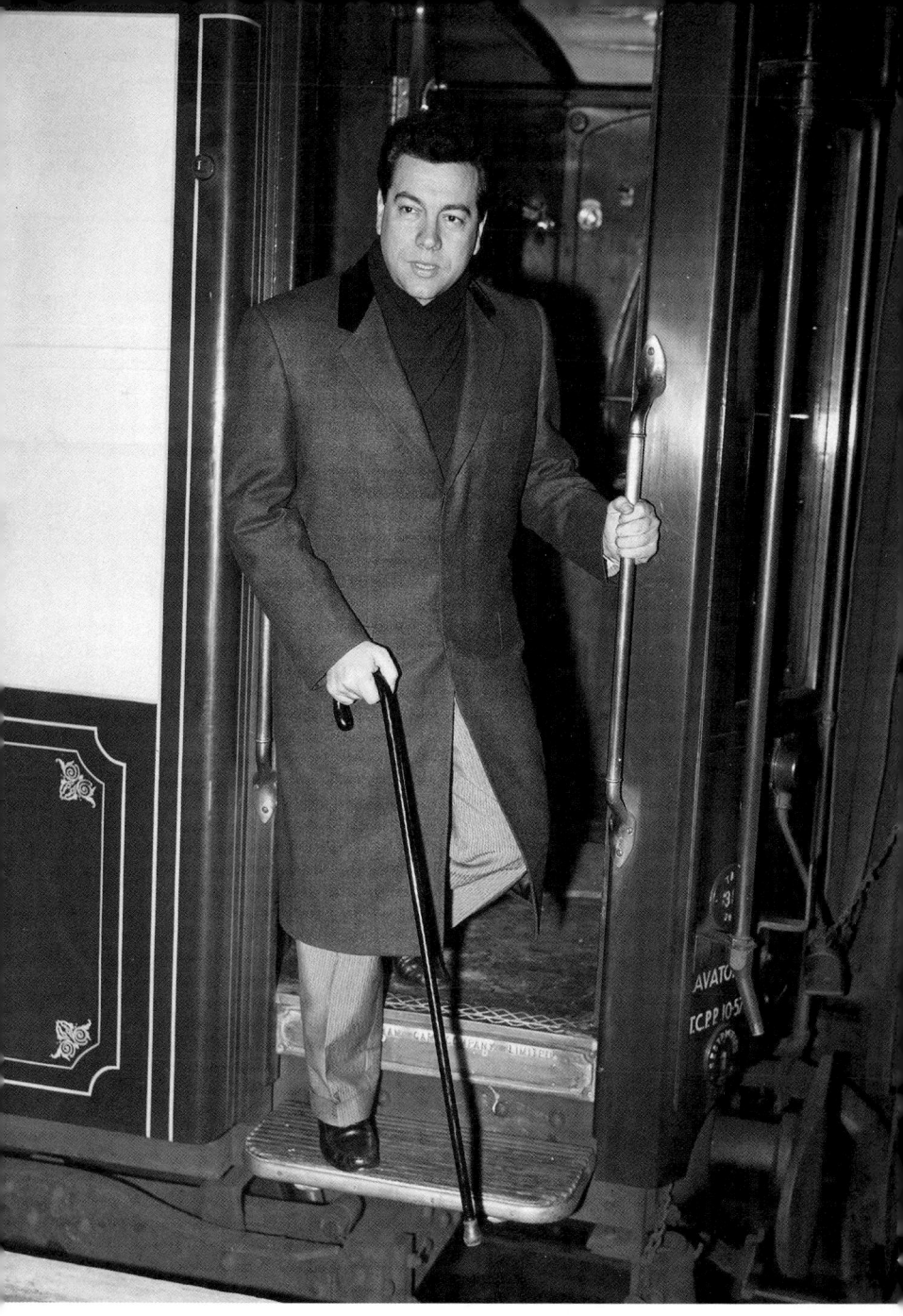

On tour for the last time, London, 1958

vuie' or 'Passione', although all twelve songs are beautifully done.[8]

In this relaxed and happy mood, Lanza celebrated the end of a remarkable year by taking Betty and the children for a Christmas vacation to San Moritz. It was destined to be their last Christmas together.

Mario Lanza's final year was plagued by ill-health and a demanding workload, mostly undertaken in the recording studio. Despite repeated warnings on his worsening state of health, the tenor continued to entertain lavishly, and the endless rounds of dinner parties at the Villa Badoglio were the talk of Rome society. He was drinking heavily again, and his singing began to suffer as a result. While RCA were at last making preparations to begin full-length operatic recordings – there was even talk of a 'special' with Maria Callas – five albums of popular songs, many of which he had recorded before, were hurried through. On practically all counts, the production of those albums left everything to be desired.

With the demand for stereophonic recordings increasing daily, RCA decided to capitalize on the new sound by having the tenor re-record some of his most famous selections in this format. Now that it was possible to record singers and orchestra on separate tracks, they also decided on a bit of technical trickery which had a further detrimental effect on the finished product.

The task of conducting for the first three albums fell to Paul Baron. They began in early 1959 with the stereo re-recordings of *The Student Prince* and *Christmas Carols* selections, and Lanza's singing was unbelievably bad. It was inconceivable that the tenor could have improved on his earlier recording of the Romberg score, but his performance with Baron at Rome's Cinecitta Studios was nothing short of a travesty. Where the original was sweet and romantic, the new recording was coarse and vulgar, the voice all but unrecognizable on most of the numbers. Indeed, the version of 'I'll Walk with God' might well serve as a 'guess-the-singer' question on a musical quiz programme, so painful is the reading. The *Christmas Carols* selection was hardly any better, the voice sullen and unfeeling on virtually every number. With loud 'scooping' notes substituting for the superbly rounded tenor heard four months earlier on the album with Ferraro, it was an astonishing turnaround. He was drinking heavily, and there were disagreements with Baron which resulted in several walkouts from their sessions together. But it was obvious too, that something more than temper was causing the change in behaviour. Lanza was desperately tired and his phlebitis continued to bother him. In April, he checked into the exclusive Valle Giulia Clinic for rest and medication under the personal supervision of Professor Guido Morica. As there was another album still to come with Baron, Callinicos left Rome for a two-month engagement with the Athens Symphony Orchestra, but he continued to keep in touch by telephone.

What Lanza thought about his work with Baron is not known, but he had performed poorly in the past with other conductors, and it seems reasonable to assume that he didn't particularly care about it one way or the other. Happily though, his third and final work with the conductor, a collection of Caruso favourites, was very much a return to form. The singing was thoughtful and well judged throughout, if still a little lacking in the sweetness and depth of feeling he had brought to the sessions with Ferraro. RCA eventually released it as part of a double album, the second record consisting of actual recordings of Caruso, which they felt would enable the listener to compare the two voices. They also invited the assistant manager of the Metropolitan Opera Company and a noted Caruso authority in his own right, Francis Robinson, to write the sleeve notes to the two collections. His assessment of Lanza's voice was particularly complimentary: 'It is not merely speaking good of the dead to say that he never sounded better than on this recording, made in Rome in June, a mere four months before he died ...[9]

By now, Callinicos had returned to Rome to find the tenor embarking, for what must have seemed the hundredth time, on a spartan diet in preparation for yet another film, *Laugh, Clown, Laugh.*

If he wanted to fulfil the movie commitments that loomed ahead, he would have to take 70 or 80 lb off his bulging frame. As he moved from one room to another in his villa, he carried a small pail with him in one hand, and a bottle of mineral water in the other. From time to time he'd take a sip of the mineral water, but he would never swallow a drop. Instead, he would spit it into the pail. It was gallingly hot that summer in Rome and denying himself water cost Mario a tremendous expense of will-power.[10]

About this time, Lanza was visited at the villa by George R. Marek, vice-president of RCA Records in New York, who discussed a number of future recordings with him, including a new album of *The Great Caruso* selections for stereo. In July, the singer's mother, Maria Lanza Cocozza, along with his grandfather, Salvatore Lanza and his Aunt Hilda all came to visit, and the entire family attended his recording of the complete *Vagabond King* selections at Cinecitta later that month. The recording also marked the return to the podium of the faithful Costa, who remarked that it was 'our best, our most harmonious session, and Mario was magnificent'.

Still, that particular recording typifies most of what was wrong with RCA's recording practice during those final sessions. What should have been a carefully paced and well-planned production, was instead completed, and poorly so, in a single five-hour session. Where the tenor in the past had concentrated on four songs to a booking, twice that number were completed in that one evening. And it showed. For example, on one of his solo numbers, 'Love Me Tonight', some of his lower notes are shaky and unsure; a fault which would have automatically necessitated a re-take had the recordings been done in America. Then too, neither the full chorus nor the soprano, Judith Raskin, who are heard singing with Lanza on the record, were present at Cinecitta; their particular contributions were dubbed on months later, in New York. It was a sloppy, careless approach to what should have been a prestigious and professional production; moreover, the recording was marred even further by poor-quality sound engineering on the part of the Rome technicians. Work had no sooner commenced on the tenor's next production, a new recording of Romberg's *The Desert Song*, than Lanza was again hospitalized at the Valle Giulia Clinic, this time suffering from pneumonia. When Callinicos visited him, he found the singer looking 'years older than his thirty-eight years'. It was August 1959, and he had less than eight weeks to live.

While Lanza was being treated at the clinic, Callinicos returned to Cinecitta and recorded the *Desert Song* selections without him. Prompted by RCA's decision to dub in the American soloists at a later date, Costa decided to do likewise with Lanza, if and when he was able to return to the studio. That particular bit of trickery would eventually ensure that the final version of *The Desert Song* went through no less than four separate recording sessions, each one re-working material completed at an earlier date. It is astonishing that the end result turned out as well as it did. Lanza's contribution to the record took place in late August, following his discharge from hospital.

> Now I started on a process of dubbing which I had never done before with Mario. With Betty in the control room, the engineer would play the record from *The Desert Song* once; Mario and I would listen intently in the studio. Then the record would be played over again, and this time Mario would sing to it, with me conducting just a few feet away. The third time Mario's voice would actually be recorded. When we were satisfied with what we'd done, we would move on to the next recording. We repeated no song more than once. After we had completed two recordings, Mario was so elated by this second-rate technique, that he asked me to make all of our future records this way.[11]

After all those wasted years in the mid-fifties, it was ironic that the tenor's busiest period of work came at a time when his health was at its worst. But despite the 'second-rate' method of completing the selections, the voice really was superb. True, his approach to some of the numbers, particularly the earlier work with Baron, left a great deal to be desired, but when his frame of reference was on target – as on a glorious 'One Alone' from *The Desert Song*, for example, or an equally mature and lyrical 'Nocturne' from *The Vagabond King* – he couldn't be faulted.

In addition to the heavy studio workload with Callinicos, Lanza was also busy with other projects. The Villa Badoglio was a hive of activity during those late summer days, as an ever-increasing list of commitments began to pile up: more session work for RCA, including the long-awaited operatic recordings; a television production for Pontiac Motors in America, to be filmed in Rome; the *Tosca* debut at the Rome Opera House and, of course, the filming of *Laugh, Clown, Laugh* for producers Alfred Panone and Irving Pisor. On 10 September 1959, Mario Lanza's final recording took place at the Cinecitta Studios.

After all their years together, it was entirely appropriate that the last work should have been with Callinicos. From the unforgettable thrill of hearing the great voice for the first time in Shippensburg; the first great recording session in New York, in 1949; to the triumphal concert tours in America and Europe, and the accolades from the Metropolitan and Rome Opera Houses; Costa had been there for them all. He had stood by too, when the troubles came: the *Student Prince* disaster which still managed to produce an unforgettable score; the lost years in the early fifties; the Chrysler show scandal and the near riots in Hamburg.

But while other singers might have been more refined, more committed to their craft and its obligations, Costa knew that the natural, God-given beauty of the Lanza voice had no peer. To be part of that gift, and the legacy that came with it was to be part of musical history. In the twelve years they had worked together, an unshakeable bond had formed between the two men, one which grew way beyond their musical commitments to one another. It was the bond of friendship and it had led them from that first meeting at a train station in Pennsylvania, all those years before, to a recording soundstage in Rome on that late summer's day in 1959.

RCA Victor had asked Mario to do some recordings for a Christmas album but somebody in the office evidently forgot to ask him to do the Malotte 'Lord's Prayer', and later, much later, they thought about it and sent him a telegram asking him to do it. However, the orchestra had already been dismissed so the next thing we could do was to go to Cinecitta and have Mario sing it to my piano accompaniment. Later we would add the orchestra in New York. So we went to Cinecitta and Mario sang 'The Lord's Prayer' very, very beautifully ... I believe the best he ever sang it in his life. So the Malotte 'Lord's Prayer' – and sometimes I think about it and I get chills – was the last thing Mario ever put down on record.[12]

Callinicos was scheduled to return to America later that day for a six-week engagement with the New York City Opera. Following a celebratory lunch of the finest black caviar, the entire Lanza family lined up outside the villa to bid safe journey to the conductor. For Callinicos, it was destined to be the final farewell to a friend. The scores for the stereophonic re-workings of *The Great Caruso* were left behind, in preparation for recordings that would never take place.

The remaining weeks in Mario Lanza's life were spent finalizing preparations for the commencement of *Laugh, Clown, Laugh*. Lanza's mother had returned to America, but Salvatore Lanza and the tenor's Aunt Hilda stayed on, as the lavish round of dinner parties continued unabated. Towards the end of September, Lanza took Betty and the children to a magnificent open-air performance of *Aïda*, at the spectacular Baths of Caracalla, in Rome. The evening came to an abrupt end, however, when he was spotted in the audience towards the end of the first act. By the time the intermission came round, the crowds surrounding him were so great that he was forced to leave. American journalist Harry Golden was seated a few rows away from him and noticed that he looked 'terribly tired'.

The final gathering at the Villa Badoglio took place on 29 September, and among the tenor's many guests that evening was an old friend from the *Winged Victory* days, Peter Lind Hayes. Hayes had his own radio programme back in California at the time and took the opportunity to record a brief interview with Lanza for the show. Their talk together took place in the library after dinner, and found the singer relaxed and happy: 'Pete, I'm going to stay here another three years at least. I love it here, I love the home I'm in. I'm very happy.' Hayes then went on to ask him about his next picture, and Lanza said: 'We're making a picture called *Laugh, Clown, Laugh* and the wonderful things that have been written in the script ... tell me that this may be the successor to *The Great Caruso*'.[13]

The following day Lanza checked in again to the Valle Giulia Clinic for further tests. He had been troubled by pains in his left side, and extensive examinations supervised this time by his personal physician, Doctor Silvestri, showed worrying signs of arterio-sclerosis. His blood pressure was high and the phlebitis continued to bother him, despite the medication. A promised appearance at a charity concert in Naples had to be cancelled, to the particular ire of one of its unnamed sponsors, Lucky Luciano. Indeed, it has been suggested by people close to Lanza that Luciano was so incensed by the tenor's failure to appear, that he subsequently ordered a 'hit' on the unfortunate man while he was receiving treatment at the clinic, by having air inserted into his bloodstream while he was sleeping. It was a subject lightly touched upon in the television documentary *Mario Lanza – an American Caruso*, but the notion seems fanciful at best.

Mafia grudge notwithstanding, it was wholly unnecessary for anyone to bear ill will toward Mario Lanza during that last week at the Valle Giulia Clinic. The damage to his system over the years, irreparable damage caused in part by his own excesses, had finally caught up with him. In the end, there was little harm that anyone could possibly do to him that had not already been done by Mario Lanza himself. At the clinic, his difficult behaviour was very much to the fore and he refused to accept the severity of the doctor's prognosis.

He received only one visitor during that time, Mrs Alfred Panone, wife of one of the co-producers of his next film, and she found him fretful and unhappy. By the time a heart specialist, Dr de la Torre, was called in, Lanza had had enough. On 6 October he informed the clinic that he was signing himself out the next day and returning to his family and his work.

In an easier frame of mind, he even consented to a brief recital for some of the nursing staff who came to see him that evening, although it would be the soft Lanza voice of 'Come Prima', rather than one of the great arias, that would be heard for the very last time in the city he had come to love. On the morning of 7 October 1959, he telephoned his wife to say he would be home later that day. A short time later, just after midday, in room 404 on the fifth floor of the clinic, Mario Lanza suffered a sudden, fatal heart attack. Despite the best efforts of Dr Silvestri and the staff, all attempts to revive him failed. Mario Lanza, the man they had called the American Caruso, was dead at the age of thirty-eight.

Despite all the warning signs that had become so increasingly evident during those last years, no one was in any way prepared for the suddenness with which it all ended. Betty Lanza was informed of her husband's death over the telephone by Doctor Silvestri; an insensitive act which at best can only be put down to the immense confusion felt by everyone at the time. She collapsed, and had to be heavily sedated during the days of grief that followed.

The singer's parents in California heard the news in an even more bizarre fashion. Terry Robinson, who was staying with the Cocozzas at the time, had the radio on over breakfast, listening to his friend's recording of 'Be My Love', when an announcer interrupted the playback to relay the tragic news from Rome. Terry had planned to spend Christmas at the Villa Badoglio and to this day still keeps the passport with the unused visa stamped across its page. Tony and Maria Cocozza were in a state of complete shock, and it was only the need to help Betty and the children which somehow managed to get them through the nightmare that followed. Maria Cocozza immediately flew to Rome – the singer's father was too ill to travel – as the first of three funeral services for her son got under way.

Lanza's body had been hurriedly and improperly embalmed and following three days of lying on view in humid heat at the villa, the first signs of deterioration were beginning to show. On 10 October, the body left the villa for the last time, for a funeral service at the Church of the Immaculate Heart of Mary, in the nearby Parioli district.

It was Rome's biggest funeral turn-out since the death of Pope Pius XII the previous year; a traditional Italian funeral procession which blocked traffic for half a mile. Thousands thronged the street, as the coffin was borne to the church in a glass-cased carriage driven by four plack-plumed horses. The immense tragedy of the occasion was overwhelming. Maria Cocozza turned to her own father and sister for whatever support and comfort they could give. Betty Lanza, her eyes hidden behind dark glasses, seemed almost in a trance, oblivious at times even to her own children, who were unable to comprehend the spectacle that surrounded them.

The family had requested that the tenor's recording of Schubert's 'Ave Maria' be played at the service, but the church authorities refused, and the hymn was sung instead by a baritone, Signor Forcioni, accompanied by the Roman Polyphonic Choir. The choice of a baritone was at least an appropriate one. No tenor alive could possibly have competed with the memory of the man whose remains rested briefly in the church that day. The Mass was said by Father Paul Maloney, a close friend of the family and the man who had baptized the four Lanza children.

It was suggested that the family might wish to have the remains interred in the Naples cemetery close to those of Caruso, but Betty Lanza would not hear of it. Following the service, attended by some of Lanza's Hollywood friends including Van Johnson, Rossano Brazzi and Xavier Cugat, the family closed up the villa and returned to America with the body. While Betty Lanza flew to California to make arrangements for her husband's final resting place, Maria Cocozza stopped off in Philadelphia, where her son's remains lay in state for twenty-four hours in Leonetti's funeral parlour, in the heart of the city.

By now the remains were grossly discoloured and distended, profoundly shocking those who had somehow expected the movie-star image to remain intact, even in death. Over 8,000 people filed past the coffin, forcing the parlour to remain open all night to accommodate the crowds. By the time the remains finally reached Los Angeles, the body was so deteriorated that the undertakers insisted it be re-identified by someone close to the immediate family. That gruesome task fell to Terry Robinson, who was horrified by what he saw. The coffin too, was starting to fall apart and a new copper casket was quickly arranged for the final service.

That final, sad farewell to Mario Lanza took place on 21 October, two weeks after his death, at the Calvary-Friedhof Church in Whittier, Los Angeles. Antonio Cocozza collapsed at his son's Mass and had to be helped from the church. Kathryn Grayson and Zsa Zsa Gabor were on hand and did what they could for the inconsolable Betty Lanza. In a way though, Betty Lanza died with her husband on that early October day in Rome. As a couple, they had more than their share of wars, as well as triumphs, and Mario Lanza's problems over the years had taken their toll on Betty as well. With Mario, the release had been sought in food and drink; with Betty, the dependence on tranquillizers had slowly become a destructive part of her lifestyle. Neither could seem to control the very weaknesses which were destroying them, but despite all of this, and perhaps, in a sad way, because of it, there was no denying the very real bond of love and affection which existed between them. It was a bond which ultimately kept them together, and kept them going.

Without Mario Lanza, life for the 36-year-old mother of his four children was just not worth living. Somehow, with the help of family and friends, she managed to get through the nightmare of those tragic days that followed his death. But when it was all over, when everyone was gone and there was nothing left but the memories, Betty Lanza too, gave up the fight.

On 11 March 1960, she was found dead in bed at her rented mansion in Beverly Hills, from what her brother Bert Hicks simply referred to as 'a broken heart'.

On that October day in Los Angeles, when the world bid its final farewell to her husband, Betty Lanza simply went through the motions. She had stood by him through all the years, bad as well as good, and she would do it yet again. For the cameras and for the public. His public. One more time.

Mario Lanza was finally laid to rest at Holy Cross Cemetery in Los Angeles, a plaintively simple inscription on his memorial plaque:

MARIO LANZA, 1921–1959

BELOVED HUSBAND AND FATHER

10   The Best of Everything

In 1982, almost a quarter of a century after Mario Lanza's untimely passing in Rome, Constantine Callinicos was asked, yet again, to describe the voice. In his time, the conductor had come to work with some of the finest vocal talents of the day, but his loyalty to his friend remained undiminished: 'It was the richest, the most expressive, the warmest, the most beautiful and satisfying, production wise, of this century that I have been able to establish.'[1]

That a voice of such magnitude was lost to classical music has long been a source of regret to serious opera lovers the world over; they feel that Mario Lanza abused a unique and truly great gift. To his many admirers however, it was a gift shared in a broader, wider fashion through his chosen career; a career which helped bring good music, and opera in particular, to a far greater audience than would have ever been possible through the inevitable confines of the opera house. Both sides of course, have a point.

Lanza's loss to the world of the great masters is well nigh inestimable, particularly when one considers the time wasted on material clearly unsuited to his highly charged talents. RCA will claim, of course, that plans were well underway in 1959 to make full-length operatic recordings. It has to be accepted too, that Lanza's own response to this part of his work was entirely wanting. A lack of resolve seemed particularly to dog him in later years when, through a combination of ill-health and indifference, he appears to have all but lost interest in the professional stage.

That indifference can also be seen in his approach to his

concert work. While never short-changing his audience when it came to intensity of performance, he did sell himself short by coasting through a repertoire that saw little development in his years as a star performer. Indeed, with the exception of one or two selections, the programme of songs presented during the early days of the 'Caruso' tour was virtually identical to that of the final concerts in Europe, in 1958. Compare that with Caruso's own catalogue of songs and arias, which changed and grew with each appearance, and some idea can be gleaned of the frustrations felt by the serious music critic, who saw it as nothing less than the tragic waste of an exceptional talent.

Lanza's relationship with his critics was almost always a stormy one. 'Lanza shouted musically'; 'Lanza emotes too much'; 'Lanza incapable of singing softly' – the war was constant and bloody. It is true, of course, that Lanza's operatic recordings are very much in the second league when compared to those of some of his modern-day counterparts. But then Mario Lanza wasn't an opera singer in the strictest sense of the word, and it was left to Callinicos to point out what should have been more obvious at the time.

> When you do a role on stage, you have to work at it so thoroughly, so much, and you have to look into every moment and every word you sing. Having done it on stage, you can then recall the feelings when you record it. Now Mario didn't have that. He didn't have that experience ... that background of having been on the stage and done it. If you look at any big star now who has done a role and does it now for recording purposes, then you can think back and re-create those emotions you felt on the stage. That's why Mario was so great and why I admire any operatic recordings that he did.[2]

Lanza's eventual sell-out to Hollywood – for that is what it was – ensured that he would never receive the acclaim he at least subconsciously sought from his peers. But it could also be said in his defence that he was the only operatically trained tenor successfully to cross that divide which separates mainstream classical music from pop.

The 'sexiest' tenor voice ever? Perhaps. Certainly it was one of the most emotionally intense and deeply felt, and if a tendency to 'over-emote' was prevalent at times – a 'rush' to the lyric that often cried out for a more restrained approach – then that too, was part of the story. But his style of singing was undeniably in a class of its own. Nobody, before or since, has ever sung quite like Mario Lanza. The urgency, that incredible 'romantic' sound that seemed to get to the very heart of the song, was at times sensational.

To the casual listener, the impact of that glorious sound was all. The fact that it was a 'tenor' voice was entirely secondary to the emotional feeling it conveyed. Lanza's tendency to go for a big finish on many of his recordings, virtually his trademark, often gave rise to complaints that he was incapable of singing softly. However, this completely overlooks his extraordinary range of singing styles, which extended far beyond those of many of his more readily acclaimed contemporaries. Listen, for example, to his recordings of such diverse numbers as Jerome Kern's 'They Didn't Believe Me' and his second version of the Schubert 'Ave Maria'. The sweetness and confidence of these recordings clearly show that Lanza could have enjoyed just as successful a career as a baritone had his top notes ever failed him.

His association with Caruso too, seemed to incense many critics, who felt it was almost blasphemous even to mention the two singers in the same breath, let alone compare them. But again, Lanza never laid claim to being another Caruso, despite occasional assertions to the contrary by the popular press. At no time, in any of his recordings, can it be said that he emulated, slavishly or otherwise, the great Italian tenor's way with a song. Lanza was very much his own man, with his own distinctive style of singing, and to his countless admirers the world over, it was more than good enough. Callinicos agreed.

> I would not actually call him another anybody, whether it is Caruso or any other artist. I would call him the artist

Mario Lanza, and he himself always begged people to think about him as an individual, who has this voice and this singing to offer ... to take him for what he is. He never compared himself to Caruso, or any other singer. He just wanted to be taken for what he is.[3]

In a professional career that spanned a mere decade, the Lanza voice left behind a remarkable legacy of unforgettable performances. Where the Caruso recordings were primitive in their early sound technique, Lanza's were fresh and clear. Where Caruso personified taste and refinement, Lanza's singing threw caution, and just about everything else, to the wind, in performances which were for the most part overwhelming in their intensity. With all that going for him, Mario Lanza couldn't possibly fail. And he didn't.

On film, *The Great Caruso* was a landmark of its kind, and there is hardly a professional opera singer alive who doesn't acknowledge some sort of debt to its all-pervading influence. Then there were the great studio performances: the entire *Student Prince* score, with Callinicos; 'Granada'; 'Valencia'; 'Song of India'; 'The Donkey Serenade'; 'Come Prima'; 'Arrivederci Roma'; 'Because'; 'Ave Maria'; and the big three-million selling singles – the list goes on and on.

His operatic recordings; if lacking in complete conviction, were still for the most part first class: the splendid *Bohème* aria from that first recording session in New York; the two *Chenier* arias recorded with Callinicos in 1950; a thrilling 'E lucevan le stelle'; the mighty *Otello* duet with Albenese; and the unforgettable *Pagliacci* aria, again with Costa, at the Rome Opera House. As long as performances such as these are played, as long as the spirit of the man is recalled through his films and his music, Mario Lanza will not be forgotten.

In the thirty years which haved passed since his death, scores of tributes and memorials have been made in the tenor's name. Not surprisingly perhaps, the singer's home town of Philadelphia is at the forefront of the honours. In

1961, Mayor Richardson Dilworth signed an official city document proclaiming 7 October Mario Lanza Memorial Day. One year later, Maria Cocozza officiated at a ceremony dedicating Mario Lanza Park at Philadelphia's 3rd and Queen Street to the memory of her son. The Settlement Music School, also on Queen Street, is the home of the city's official Mario Lanza Museum, where hundreds of photographs, records and memorabilia of his career are lovingly catalogued. A new street, Mario Lanza Boulevard, bears the singer's name in Eastwick, South West Philadelphia, while the early sixties also saw the inaugural flight on Allegheny Airlines of *The Mario Lanza*.

Fan clubs too, continue to thrive, the flagship in the UK being the British Mario Lanza Society. Apart from the usual newsletters, get-togethers and promotional work for the Lanza record releases, the society is also responsible for inaugurating the Mario Lanza Educational Foundation, a non-profit making enterprise established in 1976 for the purpose of furthering the musical education of singers by awards and scholarships in Lanza's name.

But the most enduring tribute is likely to be the work carried out in Philadelphia by the Mario Lanza Institute, chartered in 1962 by Lanza's friends and colleagues, and, like the British Educational Foundation which followed it, dedicated to perpetuating the singer's memory through the annual award of musical scholarships in his name. Many of Lanza's boyhood friends, Nicholas Petrella, Joe Curreri and Joseph Siciliano among them, play a major part in organizing the various activities of the institute, including the fund-raising Mario Lanza Ball held each year in the city.

If there is one 'father figure' overseeing and co-ordinating all the worldwide tributes to Mario Lanza, it is undoubtedly his friend and confidant, Terry Robinson. Following Betty Lanza's death in 1960, Terry took over guardianship of the four Lanza children, raising them, with the help of the tenor's parents, as his own. Today, with Callinicos, Ray Sinatra, Pasternak and Louis B. Mayer all gone, he is probably the closest remaining witness to the golden years of Mario Lanza, recalling again and again with tireless enthusiasm, the turbulent, fascinating times of the most exciting singer in the world. He is guardian not only to the tenor's children, but to the memory of the man himself.

For Mario Lanza indeed left his mark upon his times. Whether he was, or might have been, an American Caruso, is irrelevant. The body of work left behind more than stands on its own, and if there are performances too, which are less than satisfactory, then so be it. All, in their own way, help make up what was at times a complex and extraordinary career. The good, in any event, will always rise above the bad, and what seems destined to remain is the image of a dashing young man with a roguish laugh, an inestimable joy of living, and the sort of voice that comes along once in a lifetime.

Legendary voice, legendary man. Mario Lanza had it all in his time, and if it can be argued that he was his own worst enemy, it is also conversely true that he was the sole person responsible for creating that legend; a legend, moreover, that can be recalled again and again by simply putting on a recording and listening once more to that thrilling, unforgettable sound.

At the close of his weekly radio programme in the early 1950s, Mario Lanza used to sign off by wishing his listeners 'the very best of everything in life always ...' For a brief, memorable time, that just about summed up all that he himself represented. The best of times. The best of everything.

Discography: The Complete Recordings (1949–1959)

The discography on the following pages is a chronological listing of all studio performances by Mario Lanza throughout his ten-year recording career, including date and location of each take, and accompanist.

Specific recording dates are not available for the *Student Prince* and *Serenade* soundtrack collections, the numerous takes from the tenor's Coca Cola show, and a number of sessions which took place in Rome, in 1959. Most of these performances were not recorded by RCA, who instead bought them in from source (i.e. MGM, Warner Bros, and the Coca Cola Corporation).

In the case of the *Student Prince* production, this has often resulted in RCA erroneously listing Lanza's ill-fated studio work on the score, in December 1953, as the date of the actual recording (see Chapter 7, page 97). The Coca Cola songs are listed by date of broadcast only. Given that the performances were not originally intended for commercial record release (see Chapter 5, page 74), recording logs were improperly kept and were not made available to RCA. However, as the individual performances by Lanza took place within days of the actual broadcast, the dates shown are reasonably accurate. The only non-studio performance – the Albert Hall concert of January 1958 – is also included, in view of its subsequent release on record.

5 May 1949: Manhattan Center, New York: RCA Victor Orchestra; Constantine Callinicos, conductor
1 Core'ngrato'
2 *Aïda*: 'Celeste Aïda'
3 'Mama Mia che vo sape'
4 *La Bohème*: 'Che gelida manina'

23 August 1949: Republic Studios, Hollywood: RCA Victor Orchestra; Ray Sinatra, conductor
5 'They Didn't Believe Me'
6 'I Know, I Know, I Know'
7 'Mattinata'

28 October 1949: Republic Studios, Hollywood: RCA Victor Orchestra; Ray Sinatra, conductor
8 'O sole mio'
9 'Lolita'
10 'Granada'

8 April 1950: Republic Studios, Hollywood: RCA Victor Orchestra; Constantine Callinicos, conductor
11 *L'Africana*: 'O Paradiso'
12 *Carmen*: 'La Fleur que tu m'avais jetée'
13 *Carmen*: 'La Fleur que tu m'avais jetée' (Alternative take, first issued in 1981 on 'The Mario Lanza Collection')
14 *Martha*: 'M'appari'

11 April 1950: Republic Studios, Hollywood: RCA Victor Orchestra; Constantine Callinicos, conductor
15 *Madama Butterfly*: 'Stolta paura l'amor' (*with Elaine Malbin, soprano*)
16 *La Traviata*: 'Libiamo, libiamo, ne'lieti calici' (*with Elaine Malbin, soprano*)
17 *La Traviata*: 'Libiamo, libiamo, ne'lieti calici'* (*with Elaine Malbin, soprano*)
(* Alternative take, first issued in 1981 on 'The Mario Lanza Collection')

11 May 1950: Republic Studios, Hollywood: RCA Victor Orchestra; Constantine Callinicos, conductor
18 'Ave Maria' (Bach–Gounod) – violin solo by Eudice Shapiro
N.B. Miss Shapiro's solo, originally deleted by RCA for 78 rpm release, was finally restored to the tenor's recording in 1987, when it was included in the compact disc collection, Christmas with Mario Lanza

15 May 1950: Republic Studios, Hollywood: RCA Victor Orchestra; Constantine Callinicos, conductor
19 *L'Elisir d'amore*: 'Una furtiva lagrima'
20 *I Pagliacci*: 'Vesti la giubba'
21 *I Pagliacci*: 'Vesti la giubba' (alternative take, first issued in

1981 on 'The Mario Lanza Collection')
22 *Rigoletto*: 'Questa o quella'
23 *Rigoletto*: 'La Donna e mobile'

18 May 1950: Republic Studios, Hollywood: RCA Victor Orchestra; Constantine Callinicos, conductor
24 *Andrea Chenier*: 'Un di all'azzuro spazio'
25 *Andrea Chenier*: 'Come un bel di di maggio'
26 *Tosca*: 'Recondita armonia'
27 *Tosca*: 'E lucevan le stelle'

29 May 1950: Republic Studios, Hollywood: RCA Victor Orchestra; Constantine Callinicos, conductor
28 'O Holy Night'
29 *Cavalleria rusticana*: 'Addio alla madre'
30 'The Virgin's Slumber Song'
31 *Rigoletto*: 'Parmi veder le lagrime'
32 *La Gioconda*: 'Cielo e mar'

6 June 1950: Republic Studios, Hollywood: RCA Victor Orchestra; Constantine Callinicos, conductor
33 *La Forza del Destino*: 'O tu che in seno agli angeli'
34 'Serenade' (Toselli)
35 'Serenade' (Drigo)

27 June 1950: Republic Studios, Hollywood: RCA Victor Orchestra and the Jeff Alexander Choir; Ray Sinatra, conductor
36 'Tina Lina'
37 'Be My Love'

29 June 1950: Republic Studios, Hollywood: RCA Victor Orchestra and the Jeff Alexander Choir; Ray Sinatra, conductor
38 'Toast of New Orleans'
39 'Boom Biddy Boom Boom'
40 'The Bayou Lullaby'
41 'I'll Never Love You'

26 August 1950: Republic Studios, Hollywood: RCA Victor Orchestra; Ray Sinatra, conductor
42 'My Song, My Love'
43 'Because'*

44 'I Love Thee'
45 'For You Alone'*
(*Unreleased)

19 February 1951: Manhattan Center, New York: RCA Victor Orchestra; Constantine Callinicos, conductor
46 'For You Alone'
47 'Because'

23 February 1951: Manhattan Center, New York: RCA Victor Orchestra; Constantine Callinicos, conductor
48 'The Loveliest Night of the Year'
49 'A vuchella'
50 'Marechiare'

10 June 1951: Radio Recorders Studio, Hollywood: Orchestra conducted by Ray Sinatra
51 'Granada'   (Coca Cola show)
52 'Serenade' (Toselli)   (Coca Cola show)
53 'Because'   (Coca Cola show)
54 'Be My Love'   (Coca Cola show)

17 June 1951: Radio Recorders Studio, Hollywood: Orchestra conducted by Ray Sinatra
55 'Boom Biddy Boom Boom'*   (Coca Cola show)
56 'I Love Thee'*   (Coca Cola show)
57 'O sole mio'*   (Coca Cola show)
58 'The Loveliest Night of the Year'   (Coca Cola show)
(* Unreleased)

24 June 1951: Radio Recorders Studio, Hollywood: Orchestra conducted by Ray Sinatra
59 'My Song, My Love'   (Coca Cola show)
60 'Serenade' (Drigo)*   (Coca Cola show)
61 'I'll Never Love You'*   (Coca Cola show)
62 *I Pagliacci*: 'Vesti la giubba'*   (Coca Cola show)
(*Unreleased)

1 July 1951: Radio Recorders Studio, Hollywood: Orchestra conducted by Ray Sinatra
63 'Funiculi, Funicula' (English version)   (Coca Cola show)
64 'Mama mia che vo sape'*   (Coca Cola show)
65 'Someday'   (Coca Cola show)

66 'Thine Alone'   (Coca Cola show)
(*Unreleased)

8 July 1951:   Radio Recorders Studio, Hollywood: Orchestra conducted by Ray Sinatra
67 'For You Alone'*   (Coca Cola show)
68 'La danza'*   (Coca Cola show)
69 'I'm Falling in Love with Someone'   (Coca Cola show)
70 'Torna a Surriento'   (Coca Cola show)
(*Unreleased)

15 July 1951:   Radio Recorders Studio, Hollywood: Orchestra conducted by Ray Sinatra
71 'Tina Lina'   (Coca Cola show)
72 'Lolita'   (Coca Cola show)
73 *Rigoletto* – 'La Donna e mobile' (English version)*   (Coca Cola show)
74 'If'   (Coca Cola show)
(*Unreleased)

22 July 1951:   Radio Recorders Studio, Hollywood: Orchestra conducted by Ray Sinatra
75 'The World is Mine Tonight'   (Coca Cola show)
76 'Yours is My Heart Alone'   (Coca Cola show)
77 'Oh Nights of Splendour'   (Coca Cola show)
78 *Tosca*: 'Recondita Armonia'   (Coca Cola show)

29 July 1951:   Radio Recorders Studio, Hollywood: Orchestra conducted by Ray Sinatra
79 'All the Things You Are'*   (Coca Cola show)
80 'Long Ago and Far Away'   (Coca Cola show)
81 'The touch of your hand'   (Coca Cola show)
82 'The song is you'   (Coca Cola show)
(*Unreleased)

5 August 1951:   Radio Recorders Studio, Hollywood: Orchestra conducted by Ray Sinatra
83 'Cosi Cosa'   (Coca Cola show)
84 'Softly as in a Morning Sunrise'   (Coca Cola show)
85 'Diane'   (Coca Cola show)

12 August 1951:   Radio Recorders Studio, Hollywood: Orchestra conducted by Ray Sinatra

86 'A Vuchella'   (Coca Cola show)
87 'Wanting You'   (Coca Cola show)
88 'Ave Maria' (Bach-Gounod)*   (Coca Cola show)
(*Unreleased)

19 August 1951:   Radio Recorders Studio, Hollywood: Orchestra conducted by Ray Sinatra
89 'I've Got You under My Skin'   (Coca Cola show)
90 'Marechiare'   (Coca Cola show)
91 'My Heart Stood Still'   (Coca Cola show)
92 *L'Africana*: 'O Paradiso'*   (Coca Cola show)
(*Unreleased)

26 August 1951:   Radio Recorders Studio, Hollywood: Orchestra conducted by Ray Sinatra
93 'Ah Sweet Mystery of Life'   (Coca Cola show)
94 'If You are But a Dream'   (Coca Cola show)
95 'Time on My Hands'   (Coca Cola show)

2 September 1951: Radio Recorders Studio, Hollywood: Orchestra conducted by Ray Sinatra
96 'Without a Song'   (Coca Cola show)
97 'Wonder Why'   (Coca Cola show)
98 'They Didn't Believe Me'   (Coca Cola show)
99 'The Lord's Prayer'   (Coca Cola show)

9 September 1951: Radio Recorders Studio, Hollywood: Orchestra conducted by Ray Sinatra
100 'Night and Day'   (Coca Cola show)
101 'The Desert Song'   (Coca Cola show)
102 *Tosca*: 'E lucevan le stelle'   (Coca Cola show)

16 September 1951: Radio Recorders Studio, Hollywood: Orchestra conducted by Ray Sinatra
103 'With a Song in My Heart'   (Coca Cola show)
104 'Mattinata'   (Coca Cola show)

23 September 1951: Radio Recorders Studio, Hollywood: Orchestra conducted by Ray Sinatra
105 'Song of Songs'   (Coca Cola show)
106 'Strange Music'   (Coca Cola show)
107 'The Rosary'   (Coca Cola show)

28 September 1951: Republic Studios, Hollywood: RCA Victor Orchestra and the Jeff Alexander Choir; Ray Sinatra, conductor
108 'Guardian Angels'
109 'Silent Night'
110 'The First Noel'
111 'O Come All Ye Faithful'
112 'Away in a Manger'
113 'O Little Town of Bethlehem'

29 September 1951: Republic Studios, Hollywood: RCA Victor Orchestra and the Jeff Alexander Choir; Ray Sinatra, conductor
114 'We Three Kings of Orient Are'
115 'The Lord's Prayer'

22 October 1951: Radio Recorders Studio, Hollywood: Orchestra conducted by Ray Sinatra
116 'Oh Nights of Splendour'* (Coca Cola show)
(*Unreleased – alternative take to version 22 July 1951)

3 December 1951: Radio Recorders Studio, Hollywood: Orchestra conducted by Ray Sinatra
117 'Valencia' (Coca Cola show)
118 'Throught the Years' (Coca Cola show)
119 'Where or When' (Coca Cola show)
120 'None But the Lonely Heart' (Coca Cola show)

10 December 1951: Radio Recorders Studio, Hollywood: Orchestra conducted by Ray Sinatra
121 'Ay-Ay-Ay' (Coca Cola show)
122 'Look for the Silver Lining' (Coca Cola show)
123 'Your Eyes Have Told Me So' (Coca Cola show)
124 'Guardian Angels'* (Coca Cola show)
(* Unreleased)

17 December 1951: Radio Recorders Studio, Hollywood: Orchestra conducted by Ray Sinatra
125 'Ciribiribin' (Coca Cola show)
126 'Make Believe' (Coca Cola show)
127 'Sylvia' (Coca Cola show)
128 'You and the Night and the Music' (Coca Cola show)

24 December 1951: Radio Recorders Studio, Hollywood: Orchestra conducted by Ray Sinatra.
129 'O Come All Ye Faithful'* (Coca Cola show)
130 'Silent Night'* (Coca Cola show)
131 'O Little Town of Bethlehem'* (Coca Cola show)
132 'The First Noel'* (Coca Cola show)
(* Unreleased)

31 December 1951: Radio Recorders Studio, Hollywood: Orchestra conducted by Ray Sinatra
133 'Siboney' (Coca Cola show)
134 'Neapolitan Love Song' (Victor Herbert) (Coca Cola show)
135 'When Day Is Done' (Coca Cola show)

7 January 1952: Radio Recorders Studio, Hollywood: Orchestra conducted by Ray Sinatra
136 'The Best Things in Life are Free' (Coca Cola show)
137 'Temptation' (Coca Cola show)
138 'Trees' (Coca Cola show)

14 January 1952: Radio Recorders Studio, Hollywood: Orchestra conducted by Ray Sinatra/Constantine Callinicos
139 'The Donkey Serenade' (Coca Cola show)
140 'The Thrill is Gone' (Coca Cola show)
141 *Rigoletto*: 'Questa o Quella' (Callinicos) (Coca Cola show)

21 January 1952: Radio Recorders Studio, Hollywood: Orchestra conducted by Ray Sinatra
142 'Lygia' (Coca Cola show)
143 'My Romance' (Coca Cola show)
144 'The Hills of Home' (Coca Cola show)
145 'One Night of Love' (Coca Cola show)

25 January 1952: Radio Recorders Studio, Hollywood: Orchestra conducted by Ray Sinatra
146 'The Night is Young' (Coca Cola show)
147 'Somewhere a Voice is Calling' (Coca Cola show)
148 'Roses of Picardy' (Coca Cola show)
149 'Begin the Beguine' (Coca Cola show)

1 February 1952: Radio Recorders Studio, Hollywood: Orchestra conducted by Ray Sinatra
150 'Lady of Spain'   (Coca Cola show)
151 'Charmaine'   (Coca Cola show)
152 'What Is This Thing Called Love'   (Coca Cola show)
153 'I'll See You Again'   (Coca Cola show)

8 February 1952: Radio Recorders Studio, Hollywood: Orchestra conducted by Ray Sinatra/Constantine Callinicos
154 'Romance'   (Coca Cola show)
155 'Tell Me That You Love Me Tonight'*   (Coca Cola show)
156 'Among My Souvenirs'   (Coca Cola show)
157 *L'Elisir d'amore*: 'Una Furtiva Lagrima' (Callinicos) Coca Cola show)
(* Unreleased)

15 February 1952: Radio Recorders Studio, Hollywood: Orchestra conducted by Ray Sinatra
158 'I'll See You in My Dreams'   (Coca Cola show)
159 'Memories'   (Coca Cola show)
160 'I Never Knew'   (Coca Cola show)
161 'My Buddy'   (Coca Cola show)

22 February 1952: Radio Recorders Studio, Hollywood: Orchestra conducted by Ray Sinatra
162 'If I Loved You'   (Coca Cola show)
163 'Fools Rush In'   (Coca Cola show)
164 'Someday I'll Find You'   (Coca Cola show)
165 'Tell Me Tonight'   (Coca Cola show)

7 March 1952:   Radio Recorders Studio, Hollywood: Orchestra conducted by Ray Sinatra/Constantine Callinicos
166 'Yesterdays'   (Coca Cola show)
167 'Day In, Day Out'*   (Coca Cola show)
168 *Carmen*: 'La Fleur que tu m'avais jetée'* (Callinicos)   (Coca Cola show)
(* Unreleased)

14 March 1952:   Radio Recorders Studio, Hollywood: Orchestra conducted by Ray Sinatra
169 'Danny Boy'   (Coca Cola show)

170 'A Kiss in the Dark'   (Coca Cola show)
171 'The Trembling of a Leaf'   (Coca Cola show)
172 'My Wild Irish Rose'   (Coca Cola show)

21 March 1952:   Radio Recorders Studio, Hollywood: Orchestra conducted by Ray Sinatra/Constantine Callinicos
173 'Santa Lucia'*   (Coca Cola show)
174 'Just a Little Love, a Little Kiss'   (Coca Cola show)
175 *Cavalleria Rusticana*: 'Addio Alla Madre'* (Callinicos)   (Coca Cola show)
(* Unreleased)

28 March 1952:   Radio Recorders Studio, Hollywood: Orchestra conducted by Ray Sinatra/Constantine Callinicos
176 'The Moon Was Yellow'   (Coca Cola show)
177 'Core'ngrato'*   (Coca Cola show)
178 'Marcheta'   (Coca Cola show)
179 *Rigoletto*: 'La Donna e mobile' (Callinicos)   (Coca Cola show)
(* Unreleased)

4 April 1952:   Radio Recorders Studio, Hollywood: Orchestra conducted by Ray Sinatra/Constantine Callinicos
180 'April in Paris'   (Coca Cola show)
181 'Fenesta che lucive'* (Callinicos)   (Coca Cola show)
182 'And Here You Are'   (Coca Cola show)
183 *La Bohème*: 'Che gelida manina' (Callinicos)   (Coca Cola show)
(* Unreleased)

11 April 1952:   Radio Recorders Studio, Hollywood: Orchestra conducted by Ray Sinatra/Constantine Callinicos
184 'Deep in My Heart, Dear'*   (Coca Cola show)
185 'Dicitencello vuie'* (Callinicos)   (Coca Cola show)
186 'You Are Love'*   (Coca Cola show)
(* Unreleased)

18 April 1952:   Radio Recorders Studio, Hollywood: Orchestra conducted by Ray Sinatra/Constantine Callinicos
187 'Play Gypsies, Dance Gypsies'   (Coca Cola show)
188 'Maria Mari' (Callinicos)   (Coca Cola show)
189 'When You're in Love'   (Coca Cola show)
190 *La Gioconda*: 'Cielo e Mar' (Callinicos)   (Coca Cola show)

25 April 1952:   Radio Recorders Studio, Hollywood: Orchestra conducted by Ray Sinatra/Constantine Callinicos
191 'Alone Together'   (Coca Cola show)
192 'Non ti scordar di me'* (Callinicos)   (Coca Cola show)
193 *Rigoletto*: 'Parmi veder le lagrime'* (Callinicos)   (Coca Cola show)
(* Unreleased)

5 May 1952:   Radio Recorders Studio, Hollywood: Orchestra conducted by Ray Sinatra/Constantine Callinicos
194 'Beautiful Love'   (Coca Cola show)
195 'Santa Lucia luntana'* (Callinicos)   (Coca Cola show)
196 'I'll Be Seeing You'   (Coca Cola show)
197 *Aïda*: 'Celeste Aïda' (Callinicos)   (Coca Cola show)
(* Unreleased)

9 May 1952:   Radio Recorders Studio, Hollywood: Orchestra conducted by Ray Sinatra/Constantine Callinicos
198 'Love Is the Sweetest Thing'   (Coca Cola show)
199 *Andrea Chenier*: 'Come un bel di di maggio' (Callinicos)   (Coca Cola show)

16 May 1952:   Radio Recorders Studio, Hollywood: Orchestra conducted by Ray Sinatra/Constantine Callinicos
200 'You'll Never Walk Alone'*   (Coca Cola show)
201 'Na sera e maggio'* (Callinicos)   (Coca Cola show)
202 *L'Arlesiana*: 'Lamento di Federico'* (Callinicos)   (Coca Cola show)
(* Unreleased)

23 May 1952:   Radio Recorders Studio, Hollywood: Orchestra conducted by Ray Sinatra/Constantine Callinicos
203 *Andrea Chenier*: 'Un di all'azzuro spazio' (Callinicos)   (Coca Cola show)
204 'Tu Ca Nun Chiagne'* (Callinicos)   (Coca Cola show)
205 'Somebody Bigger than You and I'   (Coca Cola show)
(* Unreleased)

30 May 1952:   Radio Recorders Studio, Hollywood: Orchestra conducted by Ray Sinatra/Constantine Callinicos
206 'One Alone'   (Coca Cola show)
207 'Canta Pe Me'* (Callinicos)   (Coca Cola show)
208 *La Forza del Destino*: 'O tu che in seno agli angeli'*

(Callinicos)   (Coca Cola show)
(* Unreleased)

6 June 1952:   Radio Recorders Studio, Hollywood: Orchestra conducted by Ray Sinatra/Constantine Callinicos
209   'Besame Mucho'   (Coca Cola show)
210   'Senza Niscuino'* (Callinicos)   (Coca Cola show)
211   *Fedora*: 'Amor ti vieta'* (Callinicos)   (Coca Cola show)
(* Unreleased)

13 June 1952:   Radio Recorders Studio, Hollywood: Orchestra conducted by Ray Sinatra/Constantine Callinicos
212   'Parlami d'amore mariu' (Callinicos)   (Coca Cola show)
213   'A Kiss'   (Coca Cola show)

20 June 1952:   Radio Recorders Studio, Hollywood: Orchestra conducted by Constantine Callinicos
214   'Musica Proibita'*   (Coca Cola show)
215   *I Pagliacci*: 'Un Tal Gioco'   (Coca Cola show)
(* Unreleased)

27 June 1952:   Radio Recorders Studio, Hollywood: Orchestra conducted by Constantine Callinicos
216   'La Spagnola'   (Coca Cola show)
217   *La Bohème*: 'Testa adorata'   (Coca Cola show)

11 July 1952:   Radio Recorders Studio, Hollywood: Orchestra conducted by Ray Sinatra
218   'One Night of Love'*   (Coca Cola show)
(* Unreleased – alternative take to version of 21 January 1952)

1952:   Radio Recorders Studio, Hollywood: Orchestra conducted by Ray Sinatra
219   'Day In, Day Out' (Alternative take to version of 7 March 1952)
220   'You Are Love' (Alternative take to version of 11 April 1952)
NB: Both of these versions were chosen by RCA for record release, although neither was broadcast on the Coca Cola show. Recording dates, as such, are unknown.

24 July 1952:   Republic Studios, Hollywood: RCA Victor Orchestra conducted by Constantine Callinicos.

221   'Lee–ah–loo'
222   'You Do Something to Me'

1 August 1952:   Republic Studios, Hollywood: RCA Victor Orchestra conducted by Constantine Callinicos
223   'The Song the Angels Sing'
224   'Because You're Mine'

July/August 1952:   MGM Studios, Hollywood: Orchestra and Chorus conducted by Constantine Callinicos
225   'Serenade'
226   'Golden Days'
227   'Drink, Drink, Drink'
228   'Gaudeamus Igitur'
229   'Deep in My Heart, Dear' (with Elizabeth Doubleday, soprano)
230   'Summertime in Heidelberg' (with Elizabeth Doubleday, soprano)
231   'Beloved'
232   'I'll Walk with God'
NB: Nos. 225 to 232 inclusive are all soundtrack recordings from the MGM film 'The Student Prince'

17 June 1953:   Republic Studios, Hollywood: Orchestra and Chorus conducted by Constantine Callinicos
233   'Song of India'
234   'If You Were Mine'
235   'Call Me Fool'
236   'You Are My Love'

Summer 1955:   Warner Bros. Studio, Hollywood: Orchestra conducted by Ray Heindorf, unless otherwise noted
237   'Serenade'
238   'Serenade'* (same song, different version)
239   'La Danza' (with accordion accompaniment by Dominic Frontiere)
240   'Torna a Surriento' (with Jacob Gimpel at the piano)
241   *La Bohème*: 'O Soave Fanciulla' (with Jean Fenn, soprano; Jacob Gimpel at the piano)
242   *Der Rosenkavalier*: 'Di rigori armato' (with Jacob Gimpel at the piano)
243   *Fedora*: 'Amor ti vieta'
244   *L'Africana*: 'O Paradiso' (with Jacob Gimpel at the piano)

245 Schubert's 'Ave Maria' (with organ accompaniment)
246 *Il Trovatore*: 'Di quella pira'
247 *Otello*: 'Dio ti Giocondi' (with Licia Albenese, soprano)
248 *L'Arlesiana*: 'Lamento di Federico'
249 *Turandot*: 'Nessun dorma'
250 'My Destiny'
NB: Nos. 237 to 250 inclusive are all soundtrack recordings from the Warner Bros. film 'Serenade'.
(* Unreleased)

14 May 1956: Warner Bros. Studio, Hollywood: Orchestra and the Jeff Alexander Choir; Irving Aaronson, conductor
251 'More Than You Know'
252 'Why Was I Born?'
253 'This Nearly Was Mine'
254 'Falling in Love with Love'

15 May 1956: Warner Bros. Studio, Hollywood: Orchestra and the Jeff Alexander Choir; Irving Aaronson, conductor
255 'So in Love'
256 'Speak Low'
257 'My Romance'
258 'September Song'

17 May 1956: Warner Bros. Studio, Hollywood: Orchestra and the Jeff Alexander Choir; Irving Aaronson, conductor
259 'Younger Than Springtime'
260 'And This Is My Beloved'
261 'On the Street Where You Live'
262 'You'll Never Walk Alone'

10 August 1956: Republic Studios, Hollywood: Henri René's Orchestra and the Jeff Alexander Choir
263 'This Land'
264 'Earthbound'
265 'Deck the Halls'
266 'Hark the Herald Angels Sing'
267 'God Rest Ye Merry Gentlemen'
268 'Joy to the World'

15 August 1956: Republic Studios, Hollywood: Henri René's Orchestra and the Jeff Alexander Choir
269 'O Christmas Tree'

270 'I Saw Three Ships'
271 'Love in a Home'
272 'Do You Wonder'
273 'It Came Upon a Midnight Clear'

27 August 1956: Republic Studios, Hollywood: Henri René's Orchestra and the Jeff Alexander Choir
274 'I've Told Ev'ry Little Star'
275 'Only a Rose'
276 'Will You Remember'

31 August 1956: Republic Studios, Hollywood: Henri René's Orchestra and the Jeff Alexander Choir
277 'Rose Marie'
278 'The Donkey Serenade'
279 'All the Things You Are'
280 'Gypsy Love Song'

6 September 1956: Republic Studios, Hollywood: Henri René's Orchestra and the Jeff Alexander Choir
281 'Lover Come Back to Me'
282 'Tramp! Tramp! Tramp!'
283 'Giannina Mia'
284 'Thine Alone'*
285 'Yours Is My Heart Alone'
NB * *Song nos. 274 to 285 inclusive were originally issued by RCA on an album entitled 'A Cavalcade of Show Tunes'. For some unknown reason however, the tenor's dramatic 'high C' conclusion to 'Thine Alone' was omitted from the album and the complete version of the song, as originally recorded, did not appear until 1968, when it was included in the collection 'The Best of Mario Lanza Vol. 2'*

15 April 1957: Republic Studios, Hollywood: Henri René's Orchestra and the Jeff Alexander Choir
286 'A Night to Remember'
287 'Behold'
288 'Come Dance with Me'

June 1957: Auditorium Angelico, Rome: Orchestra and Chorus conducted by George Stoll/Silvio Clemintelli
289 'Seven Hills of Rome'
290 'There's Gonna Be a Party Tonight'
291 'Lolita'

292   'Arrivederci Roma' (with Luisa di Mio)
293   'Come Dance with Me'
294   *Imitation sequence*: 'Temptation'; 'Jezebel'; 'Memories are Made of This' and 'When the Saints Go Marching In'.
295   *Rigoletto*: 'Questa o Quella'* (Clemintelli)
(* Unreleased – 1950 recording used on soundtrack album)
NB Nos. 289 to 294 inclusive are all soundtrack recordings from the MGM film 'Seven Hills of Rome'.

7 November 1957: Cinecitta Studios, Rome: Orchestra conducted by George Stoll
296   'The Loveliest Night of the Year'
297   'Arrivederci Roma' (English version)
298   'Younger Than Springtime'
299   'Never Till Now'

16 January 1958:   Concert at the Royal Albert Hall, London: Constantine Callinicos at the piano
300   *L'Arlesiana*: 'Lamento di Federico'
301   'Lasciatemi Morire'*
302   'Gia il sole del gange'
303   'Pieta signore'
304   'Tell Me O Blue Blue Sky'
305   'Bonjour ma belle'
306   'The House on the Hill'
307   *Tosca*: 'E lucevan le stelle'
308   'Mama mia che vo sape'
309   'A Vuchella'
310   'Marechiare'
311   'Softly as in a Morning Sunrise'
312   'I'm Falling in Love with Someone'
313   'Because You're Mine'
314   'Seven Hills of Rome'
315   *Rigoletto*: 'La Donna e mobile'*
(* Unreleased)

June 1958:   Cinecitta Studios, Rome: Orchestra conducted by Carlo Savina/George Stoll
316   'O sole mio'
317   'Come prima'
318   'O mon amour'
319   Schubert's 'Ave Maria' (Stoll)

Late August 1958:   The Rome Opera House: Orchestra, Chorus and Soloists; Constantine Callinicos, conductor
320   *Aïda*: 'Grand March'
321   *Otello*: 'Nium mi tema'
322   *I Pagliacci*: 'Vesti la giubba'
323   *Cosi Fan Tutti*: Trio*
324   'I Love Thee'
(* Unreleased)

November 1958:   Berlin, Germany: Johannes Rediske and his band
325   'Hofbrauhaus Song'
326   'Pineapple Pickers'
NB: *Nos. 316 to 326 inclusive are all soundtrack recordings from the MGM film* 'For the First Time'

November/December 1958:   Cinecitta Studios, Rome: Orchestra conducted by Franco Ferrara/chorus by Franco Potenza
327   'Funiculi, funicula'
328   'Dicitencello vuie'
329   'Maria Mari'
330   'Voce 'e notte'
331   'Canta pe'mme'
332   'O surdato 'namurato'
333   'Come facette mammeta'
334   'Santa Lucia luntana'
335   'Fenesta che lucive'
336   'Tu ca nun chiagne'
337   ' 'Na sera e maggio'
338   'Passione'

April 1959:   Cinecitta Studios, Rome: Orchestra conducted by Paul Baron. Chorus added later in New York.
339   'Resta cu' me'*
340   'Volare'*
341   'Guaglione'*
342   'Strada 'nfosa'*
343   'Come prima' (different version to film soundtrack)*
344   'Summertime in Heidelberg' (with Norma Giusti, soprano)
345   'Gaudeamus Igitur'
346   'Just We Two' (with Norma Giusti, soprano)

(* Unreleased)

347 'Thoughts Will Come Back to Me'
348 'Golden Days'
349 'I'll Walk with God'
350 'Serenade'
351 'Beloved'
352 'Drink, Drink, Drink.'
353 'Deep in My Heart, Dear' (with Norma Giusti, soprano)
NB: Nos. 344 to 353 inclusive are from stereophonic re-recordings of 'The Student Prince'

May 1959: Cinecitta Studios, Rome: Orchestra conducted by Paul Baron. Chorus added later in New York.
354 'We Three Kings of Orient Are'
355 'O Come All Ye Faithful'
356 'O Little Town of Bethlehem'
357 'The First Noel'
358 'Silent Night'
359 'Away in a Manger'
360 'Guardian Angels'
361 'Joy to the World'
362 'Hark the Herald Angels Sing'
363 'It Came upon a Midnight Clear'
364 'God Rest Ye Merry Gentlemen'
365 'O Christmas Tree'
366 'Deck the Halls'
367 'I Saw Three Ships'
NB: Nos. 354 to 367 inclusive are stereophonic re-recordings issued as 'Lanza Sings Christmas Carols'.

June 1959: Cinecitta Studios, Rome: Orchestra conducted by Paul Baron
368 'Vieni sul mar'
369 'Senza nisciuno'
370 'Musica Proibita'
371 'Vaghissima Sembianza'
372 'Serenata'
373 'Lolita'
374 'Luna d'estate'
375 'L'alba separa dalla luce l'ombra'
376 'Pour un baiser'
377 'La mia canzone'
378 'Ideale'
379 'Santa Lucia'

July 1959: Cinecitta Studios, Rome: Orchestra conducted by Constantine Callinicos (Chorus and soloist added later in New York)

380 'Love Me Tonight'
381 'Tomorrow' (with Judith Raskin, soprano)
382 'Drinking Song'
383 'Nocturne'
384 'Song of the Vagabonds'
385 'Finale – Only a Rose' (with Judith Raskin, soprano)
386 'Only a Rose' (with Judith Raskin, soprano)
387 'Someday' (with Judith Raskin, soprano)
NB: Nos. 380 to 387 inclusive are all from 'The Vagabond King'

August 1959: Cinecitta Studios, Rome: Orchestra conducted by Constantine Callinicos. Chorus and soloists added later in New York.

388 'Then you will know' (with Judith Raskin, soprano)
389 'Riff Song'
390 'My Margo'*
391 'The Desert Song' (with Judith Raskin, soprano)
392 'One Flower in your garden' (with Donald Arthur, bass)
393 'One Alone'
394 'One Alone' (Reprise)
395 'Azuri's dance'
396 'I want a kiss' (with Judith Raskin, soprano and Raymond Murcell, baritone)
397 'One good boy gone wrong' (with Judith Raskin, soprano)
(* Unreleased)
NB: Excluding nos. 390 and 394, all the above were issued on the album The Desert Song. *The abbreviated reprise of* 'One Alone' *(no. 394) was not included in the original release and turned up instead on* The Mario Lanza Collection *issued in 1981.*

10 September 1959: Cinecitta Studios, Rome: Constantine Callinicos at the piano.

398 'The Lord's Prayer'*
(* Unreleased)

Filmography

Production details of Mario Lanza's seven films are listed overleaf. *The Student Prince*, for which his singing voice only was used, is also included. Details of songs and arias featured in the tenor's first four films are shown also, as none of these performances was commercially released on record. From *The Student Prince* onwards, RCA issued the actual soundtrack performances on disc, a listing of which can be found in the Discography.

Lanza also appeared in the chorus of *Winged Victory* (20th Century Fox, 1944 – see Stage, Radio and Television Appearances) but is not identifiable on screen.

THAT MIDNIGHT KISS (1949) MGM

Director: Norman Taurog; *Producer*: Joe Pasternak; *Screenplay*: Bruce Manning, Tamara Hovey; *Musical Director*: Charles Previn; *Running Time*: 98 minutes; *Technicolor*.

Cast: Kathryn Grayson, José Iturbi, Ethel Barrymore, Keenan Wynn, J. Carrol Naish, Jules Munshin, Thomas Gomez, Marjorie Reynolds and 'introducing' Mario Lanza.

Songs: 'Mama mia che vo sape; *L'Elisir D'Amore*: 'Una furtiva lagrima'; *Aïda*: 'Celeste Aïda'; 'They Didn't Believe Me'*; 'I Know, I Know, I Know'; 'Love Is Music'*

(* *Duet with Kathryn Grayson*)

NB An additional song, 'One Love of Mine', based on a movement from Tchaikovsky's Piano Concerto in B Flat Minor, was also sung as a duet by Lanza and Grayson, but was not used in the film's final print.

THE TOAST OF NEW ORLEANS (1950) MGM

Director: Norman Taurog; *Producer*: Joe Pasternak; *Screenplay*: Sy Gomberg, George Wells; *Musical Directors*: George Stoll and Johnny Green; *Running Time*: 97 minutes; *Technicolor*.

Cast: Kathryn Grayson, Mario Lanza, David Niven, J. Carrol Naish, Richard Hageman, James Mitchell.

Songs: 'The Toast of New Orleans'; 'Be My Love'*; 'Tina Lina'; 'Boom Biddy Boom Boom'; *Carmen*: 'La Fleur que tu m'avais jetée'; *L'Africana*: 'O Paradiso'; *Martha*: 'M'appari; 'I'll Never Love You'; *La Traviata*: 'Libiamo libiamo ne 'lieti calici'*; 'The Bayou Lullaby'*; *Madama Butterfly*: 'Stolta paura l'amor'*.
(* *Duet with Kathryn Grayson*)
NB 'Be My Love' was nominated for an Academy Award in the 'Best Song' category, but lost out to 'Mona Lisa'.

THE GREAT CARUSO (1951) MGM
Director: Richard Thorpe; *Producer*: Joe Pasternak; *Screenplay*: Sonya Levien, William Ludwig; *Musical Directors*: Johnny Green, Peter Herman Adler; *Running Time*: 109 minutes; *Technicolor*.
Cast: Mario Lanza, Ann Blyth, Dorothy Kirsten, Jarmila Novotna, Carl Benton Reid, Eduard Franz, Richard Hageman, Ludwig Donath, Alan Napier.
Songs: 'Marechiare'; 'A vuchella'; 'La Danza'; *Cavalleria Rusticana*: 'No, Turiddu, rimani' (with Marina Koshetz); *La Gioconda*: 'Cielo e mar'; *Rigoletto*: 'La Donna e mobile'; *Aïda*: 'Celeste Aïda'; 'Torna a Surriento'; *Aïda*: 'O terra addio' (with Dorothy Kirsten and Blanche Thebom); *La Bohème*: 'Che gelida manina'; 'Mattinata'; *Il Trovatore*: 'Ah, madre, addio' (with Lucine Amara); *Rigoletto*: 'Quartet' (with Blanche Thebom, Olive Mae Beach and Guiseppe Valdengo); *Tosca*: 'E lucevan le stelle'; *Cavalleria Rusticana*: 'Brindisi'; *I Pagliacci*: 'Vesti la giubba'; Bach-Gounod 'Ave Maria'; *Lucia Di Lammermoor*: 'Sextet' (with Dorothy Kirsten, Blanche Thebom, Gilbert Russell, Nicola Moscona and Guiseppe Valdengo); 'Because'; *Martha*: 'M'appari'; *Martha*: 'Finale' (with Dorothy Kirsten, Blanche Thebom and Nicola Moscona).
NB 'The Loveliest Night of the Year' was also featured in the picture, sung on-screen by Ann Blyth. The Great Caruso won an Academy Award for the best sound recording, the Oscar going to Douglas Shearer. Peter Herman Adler and Johnny Green were also nominated for scoring for a musical picture, along with Helen Rose and Gil Steele for costume and design. The awards for both these categories however, lost out to An American in Paris.

BECAUSE YOU'RE MINE (1952) MGM
Director: Alexander Hall; *Producer*: Joe Pasternak; *Screenplay*: Leonard Spiegelgass, Karl Tunberg; *Musical Director*: Johnny Green; *Running Time*: 103 minutes; *Technicolor*.

Cast: Mario Lanza, Doretta Morrow, James Whitmore, Paula Corday, Jeff Donnell, Spring Byington.
Songs: Cavalleria Rusticana: 'Addio alla madre' (with Peggy Bonni and Kathryn Chapman); 'Mama mia che vo sape'; *Rigoletto*: 'Questa o quella'; 'The Song the Angels Sing'; 'Lee-ah-loo'; 'The Lord's Prayer'; 'Because You're Mine'*; *Rigoletto*: 'Addio, addio' (with Paula Corday); *L'Africana*: 'O Paradiso'; 'Granada'.

(* *Duet with Doretta Morrow*)

NB *'Because You're Mine' was nominated for an Academy Award in the 'Best Song' category, but lost out to the theme song from* High Noon.

THE STUDENT PRINCE (1954) MGM
Director: Richard Thorpe; *Producer*: Joe Pasternak; *Screenplay*: William Ludwig, Sonya Levien; *Musical Director*: George Stoll; *Running Time*: 107 minutes; *Anscolour*.
Cast: Ann Blyth, Edmund Purdom, Edmund Gwenn, S.Z. Sakall, John Williams, John Ericson, Louis Calhern, and 'the singing voice of Mario Lanza'.
Songs: For complete listing, see under Discography, page 150.

SERENADE (1956) Warner Bros
Director: Anthony Mann; *Producer*: Henry Blanke; *Screenplay*: Ivan Goff, Ben Roberts: Based upon the novel by James M. Cain; *Musical Director*: Ray Heindorf; *Running Time*: 121 minutes; *Warnercolour*.
Cast: Mario Lanza, Joan Fontaine, Sarita Montiel, Vincent Price, Joseph Callelia, Harry Bellaver, Vince Edwards.
Songs: For complete listing, see under Discography, page 150.

SEVEN HILLS OF ROME (1957) MGM/Titanus
Director: Roy Rowland; *Producer*: Lester Welch; *Screenplay*: Art Cohn, Giorgio Prosperi; *Musical Director*: George Stoll; *Running Time*: 104 minutes; *Technirama*.
Cast: Mario Lanza, Renato Rascel, Marisa Allasio, Peggy Castle.
Songs: In addition to the songs listed in the Discography, pages 152–3, Lanza is also heard in two brief excerpts, 'All the Things You Are' and 'The Loveliest Night of the Year'.

FOR THE FIRST TIME (1959) MGM/Corona Orion
Director: Rudolph Maté; *Producer*: Alexander Gruter; *Screenplay*:

Andrew Solt; *Musical Director*: George Stoll; *Running Time*: 97 minutes; *Technirama*.

Cast: Mario Lanza, Johanna von Koczian, Kurt Kasznar, Zsa Zsa Gabor.

Songs: For a complete listing, see Discography, pages 153–4.

Stage, Radio and Television Appearances

The following stage (S), radio (R) and television (TV) appearances by Mario Lanza throughout his career, are listed in chronological order.

Details of songs performed at his early concert appearances are incomplete, but subsequent radio performances, as well as stage and television appearances from 1947 onwards, are fully listed.

7 August 1942: (S) Berkshire Music Festival, Tanglewood, Massachusetts
Graduation performance as Fenton, in Otto Nicolai's comic opera, *The Merry Wives of Windsor* (Boris Goldovsky, conductor).

Summer 1943: (S) *On the Beam*. Musical army revue by Peter Lind Hayes and Frank Loesser
The revue toured army bases throughout the United States, and featured Lanza in a comic take-off of the bullfighter aria from Bizet's *Carmen*.

20 November 1943: (S) *Winged Victory*, 44th Street Playhouse, New York
Play-cum-musical by Moss Hart, which ran on Broadway for 212 performances. Lanza was part of a fifty-man choral group under the direction of Lieut. Leonard de Paur. Lanza was also on hand for the filming of the play in 1944, under the direction of George Cukor.

24 October 1945: (R) *The Celanese Hour*: 'Great Moments in Music' (Sylvan Levin, conductor)
Excerpts from *Tosca*. Lanza sings 'E lucevan le stelle', 'Recondita

161

armonia' (with Robert Weede, baritone) and 'Love Duet' (with Jean Tennyson, soprano).

7 November 1945: (R) *The Celanese Hour*: 'Great Moments in Music' (Burgess Meredith, narrator)
Lanza sings 'The House on the Hill' and 'America the Beautiful' (with Robert Weede, baritone, and Vivian Bauer, soprano).

14 November 1945: (R) *The Celanese Hour*: 'Great Moments in Music' (George Sebastian, conductor)
Lanza sings 'Drinking Song' (with Robert Weede, baritone) and the 'Love Duet' (with Jean Tennyson, soprano) from Verdi's *Otello*.

19 December 1945: (R) *Red Barber Review*
Lanza sings 'Vesti la giubba' and 'I'm Falling in Love with Someone'.

26 December 1945: (R) *The Celanese Hour*: 'Great Moments in Music' (George Sebastian, conductor)
Excerpts from Lehmann's *In a Persian Garden*. Lanza sings 'A Jug of Wine' (with Frances Yeend, soprano) and 'Ah Moon of My Delight'.

Lanza also toured Canada in 1945 for a number of concert appearances with Agnes Davis, soprano, and pianist Josef Blatt.

2 January 1946: (R) *The Celanese Hour*: 'Great Moments in Music' (Sylvan Levin, conductor)
The Music of Irving Berlin. Lanza sings 'A Pretty Girl Is Like a Melody', 'Blue Skies' (with Natalie Bodanya, soprano) and 'All Alone'/'What'll I Do' (with Bodanya and Leonard Stokes, baritone).

20 February 1946: (R) *The Celanese Hour*: 'Great Moments in Music' (Sylvan Levin, conductor)
Excerpts from Romberg's *The Student Prince*. Lanza sings 'Serenade', 'Deep in My Heart, Dear' (with Winifred Smith, soprano) and 'Golden Days' (with Robert Weede, baritone).

Lanza was also booked to sing excerpts from *Die Fledermaus*, 'Mignon' and *La Traviata* on a further three *Celanese* programmes, but cancelled the appearances. (See Chapter 2, page 29.)

14 April 1947: (S) State Teachers' College Auditorium, Shippensburg, Pennsylvania
Lanza's first recital with Constantine Callinicos.

8 July 1947: (S) First concert of The Bel Canto Trio with Frances Yeend, soprano and George London, bass-baritone.
The Trio gave eighty-six concerts in all between July 1947 and 27 May 1948, including appearances at Milwaukee; Ames, Iowa; Minot, North Dakota; La Porte, Indiana; Albion, Michigan; Middletown, New York; Sylacauga, Alabama; Wallingford, Connecticut; and Chihuahua, Mexico.

A typical Bel Canto Trio performance consisted of the following selections:

'Qual volutta trascorer', from Verdi's *I Lombardi* (Lanza, Yeend and London).

'In felice, e tuo credevi' from Verdi's *Ernani* and 'Quand la flamme de l'amour' from Bizet's *La Jolie Fille de Perth* (London).

'Parigi O cara' from Verdi's *La Traviata* (Lanza and Yeend).

'In quelle trine morbide' from Puccini's *Manon Lescaut* and the 'Jewel Song' from Gounod's *Faust* (Yeend).

'Ecco il magico liquore' from Donizetti's *L'Elisir d'Amore* (Lanza and London).

'E lucevan le stelle' from Puccini's *Tosca* and 'M'appari' from Flotow's *Martha* (Lanza).

'Legères hirondelles' from Thomas's *Mignon* (Yeend and London).

'Perdon, perdon Amelia' from Verdi's *Simon Boccanegra* (Lanza, Yeend and London).

Following an intermission, the trio would conclude with:

'Farewell scene' from Mozart's *The Magic Flute* (Lanza, Yeend and London).

'La Donna e mobile' from Verdi's *Rigoletto* (Lanza).

'Nobody Could Love You More' from Lehar's *Paganini* (Lanza and Yeend).

'Musetta's Waltz' from Puccini's *La Bohème* (Yeend).

'Bess You Is My Woman Now' from Gershwin's *Porgy and Bess* (London and Yeend).

'Prison Scene' from Gounod's *Faust* (Lanza, Yeend and London).

28 August 1947: (S) Hollywood Bowl Concert, Eugene Ormandy conducting
Lanza sings 'Una furtiva lagrima' from Donizetti's *L'Elisir d'Amore*; 'Un di all'azzuro spazio' from Giordano's *Andrea Chenier*; 'E lucevan le stelle' from *Tosca*; the Love Duet from *Madama Butterfly* (with Frances Yeend, soprano) and 'O soave Fanciulla' from *La Bohème* (also with Yeend).
The concert was also recorded for NBC radio.

14 February 1948: (R) Edgar Bergin/Charlie McCarthy Show from Fair Park Auditorium, Dallas, Texas
Lanza sings 'Vesti la giubba' from *I Pagliacci*.

7/8 April 1948: (S) Municipal Auditorium, St Louis. Two performances of Puccini's *Madama Butterfly* by the.New Orleans Opera House Association, under the direction of Walter Herbert
Lanza's professional operatic debut, as Lieut. Pinkerton, with Tomiko Kanazawa as Cio Cio San and Jess Walters as Sharpless.

18 June 1948: (R) Final, one-off appearance of The Bel Canto Trio
They sang an excerpt from Act Four of Puccini's *La Bohème*, in English, as part of a demo disc for a proposed NBC opera programme. (See Chapter 3, page 38.)

24 July 1948: (S) MGM Night, Hollywood ˙ Bowl. Eugene Ormandy, conductor
Lanza sings 'Agnus Dei'; 'O soave Fanciulla' from *La Bohème* (with Kathryn Grayson, soprano); Victor Herbert's 'Thine Alone' (also with Grayson); 'Nessun dorma' from *Turnadot* and the 'Hallowe'en Suite' with Grayson and basso Lee Wintner.
The concert was also recorded for NBC radio.

22 September 1948: (R) *Salute to MGM*
'Live' broadcast. Lanza sings 'Thine Alone'.

25 November 1948: (R) Elgin Watch Thanksgiving Special: *Two Hours of Stars* (Don Ameche, host)
Lanza sings 'Cosi cosa'; 'E lucevan le stelle' from *Tosca* and the Thanksgiving hymn, 'All Ye Thankful People Come'. Broadcast live on NBC.

December 1948: (R) Second Edgar Bergin/Charlie McCarthy Show
Lanza sings 'The Lord's Prayer'.

March/May 1949: (S) Concert tour with Callinicos
Venues include Clinton, Iowa; Zanesville, Ohio; Athens, Ohio; Wilmington, Delaware; Troy, New York; Portland, Maine; Fort Wayne, Indiana; Duluth, Minnesota; Chicago; Minneapolis; New Orleans; Tulsa, Oklahoma; Sylcauga, Alabama; and Centralia, Illinois.

16 August 1949: (S) MGM Programme, Hollywood Bowl. Johnny Green, conductor
Lanza sings 'Celeste Aïda' from Verdi's *Aïda*, and 'Addio, addio' from *Rigoletto* (with Mary Jane Smith, soprano). Broadcast live on NBC.

29 September 1949: (R) Screen Guild Theatre Programme
Special with Kathryn Grayson to promote *That Midnight Kiss*. Songs featured: 'Mama mia che vo sape'; 'They Didn't Believe Me' (duet with Grayson); 'I Know, I Know, I Know'; and 'Verranno a te sull'aure' from *Lucia di Lammermoor* (also with Grayson). Broadcast on NBC. Lanza and Grayson also toured a number of venues throughout the United States at which they performed one or two songs from the film. (See Chapter 4, page 48.)

1950: (S) Three concerts at the High School Auditorium, in Honolulu, Hawaii, accompanied by Constantine Callinicos (piano)

April 1950: (S) Charity Show, *Friars' Frolics*, from the Shrine Auditorium, Los Angeles
Lanza sings 'Vesti la giubba'.

February 1951: Nationwide, twenty-concert tour with Callinicos
Utica, New York; Baltimore; Richmond, Virginia; Columbus, Ohio; Philadelphia Academy of Music; Miami Beach; Orlando, Florida; Daytona Beach, Florida; St Louis; Milwaukee; Toledo; Cincinatti; Wichita; Kansas City; Omaha, Nebraska; Ogden, Utah; Tampa; New Orleans; Chicago and Fresno, California.
For programme of songs, see Chapter 4 pages 60–1.

6 March 1951: (S) Syria Mosque, Pittsburgh. Pittsburgh Symphony Orchestra conducted by Vladimir Bakaleinikoff
Audience also admitted to afternoon rehearsal (see Chapter 4, page 61).

10 June 1951: (R) *The Mario Lanza Show* sponsored by Coca Cola debuts on CBS
Sixty-nine shows in all are broadcast up to September 1952; the first seventeen with CBS and the remainder with NBC. Conducting honours alternate between Ray Sinatra and Callinicos. For complete listing of all performances by Lanza, see Discography.

30 September 1954: (TV) *Shower of Stars* show sponsored by Chrysler Motors
Live TV show. Lanza mimes to three previously recorded numbers: 'Be My Love'; 'Marechiare' and 'Vesti la giubba'.

28 October 1954: (TV) *Shower of Stars*
Second Chrysler show. Lanza sings live: 'E lucevan le stelle' from *Tosca* and 'Someday', from *The Vagabond King*.

July 1957: Charity concert, Naples, Italy
Lanza broke off filming *Seven Hills of Rome* to make a brief appearance at this concert. Believed to have sung 'Be My Love', 'Santa Lucia' and 'O Sole Mio'.

31 October 1957: (TV) *The Christopher Programme.* **Paul Baron, piano**
Filmed in Rome for subsequent broadcast on American television, Mario and Betty Lanza discuss their life and the singer's career with Father Keller, founder of the Christophers, a Catholic charity organization. Lanza sings three songs:

Schubert's 'Ave Maria'; 'Because You're Mine' and 'Santa Lucia', accompanied by Baron on piano.

16 November 1957: (S) Royal Variety Performance, London Palladium. Orchestra conducted by Constantine Callinicos

Lanza sings 'Because You're Mine'; 'E lucevan le stelle' and 'The Loveliest Night of the Year' for Queen Elizabeth and Prince Philip of England. (Edited highlights broadcast on radio three days later.)

24 November 1957: (TV) *Sunday Night at the London Palladium.* **Orchestra conducted by Callinicos**

Same selection of songs as Command Performance. Broadcast on ATV Television.

4 January 1958: (S) European concert tour. Constantine Callinicos, piano

Appearances at Sheffield; Glasgow, Scotland; Newcastle (2); Leicester (2); Royal Albert Hall (2); Bristol; Manchester; Brighton; Edinburgh, Scotland; Dundee, Scotland; Munich, West Germany; Belfast, N. Ireland; Paris, France; Rotterdam and Hanover.

Lanza's first appearance at the Albert Hall on 16 January was recorded by RCA and subsequently released on record. (See Discography.)

18 January 1958: (TV) *Saturday Night Spectacular,* introduced by David Jacobs and broadcast on ATV Television. **Constantine Callinicos at the piano**

Lanza sings three numbers: 'Softly As in a Morning Sunrise'; 'Marechiare' and 'I'm Falling in Love With Someone'.

13 April 1958: (S) Osterhalle, Kiel, West Germany. Constantine Callinicos at the piano

Lanza's final public appearance in concert.

Notes

Chapter 1
1. Peter Herman Adler, notes from *Mario Lanza – A Legendary Performer* (RCA Records, 1976).
2. Constantine Callinicos, radio interview, Columbus, Ohio, June 1974. Courtesy British Mario Lanza Society.
3. Joseph Siciliano, interview with Richard Stevenson for British Mario Lanza Society, 1980.
4. Lanza, interview for Berlin radio, 1958.
5. Noel Straus, *New York Herald Tribune*, 8 August 1942.

Chapter 2
1. Jerry Adler, letter to Stephen Pattinson, 17 May 1976.
2. Frank Sinatra, Columbia Concerts Inc., press release. NYC 1945.
3. Lanza, interview with Hedda Hopper, 1948.
4. Constantine Callinicos, *The Mario Lanza Story* (Coward-McCann Inc., New York 1960).
5. Ibid.
6. Hermann Hausner, *Tragodie einer Stimme* (Documenten-Verlag Books, Munich, 1962).
7. *Etude* magazine, 'My First Big Opportunity' (December 1949).
8. Ibid.
9. Gilles Mercier, *Quebec News Review*, 11 October 1945.
10. Letter from W. Kilpatrick, Coronet Concerts and Artists, Ontario, to Ada Cooper, Columbia Concerts Inc., New York, dated 14 November 1946. (Courtesy British Mario Lanza Society).
11. Callinicos, *The Mario Lanza Story*.
12. Ibid.
13. Callinicos, radio interview, Columbus, Ohio, June 1974. Courtesy British Mario Lanza Society.

Chapter 3
1. Halline, *Milwaukee Sentinel*, 9 July 1947.
2. Davis, *Milwaukee Journal*, 9 July 1947.
3. Claudia Cassidy, *Chicago Tribune*, 20 July 1947.
4. Callinicos, *The Mario Lanza Story*.
5. Ibid.
6. *Los Angeles Times*, 29 August 1947.
7. *Los Angeles Daily News*, 29 August 1947.
8. *The Mario Lanza Story*, BBC radio, March 1974.
9. Laurence Oden, *St Louis News*, 9 April 1948.
10. Lanza, interview with Hedda Hopper, 1948.
11. Callinicos, *The Mario Lanza Story*.
12. Callinicos, radio interview, Columbus, Ohio, June 1974. Courtesy British Mario Lanza Society.

Chapter 4
1. Richard Mohr, notes from *The Mario Lanza Collection*, RCA Records, 1981.
2. Bosley Crowther, *New York Times*, 28 February 1949.
3. Terry Robinson, *The Mario Lanza Story*, BBC radio, March 1974.
4. Sammy Cahn, *I Should Care – The Sammy Cahn Story*, (W. H. Allen, 1975).
5. Joe Pasternak, *The Mario Lanza Story*, BBC radio, March 1974.
6. Peter Herman Adler, *Mario Lanza – An American Caruso*, 1983, Producer: Jo Ann Young.
7. *New York Herald Tribune*, May 1951.
8. *New York Times*, May 1951.
9. *Variety*, May 1951.
10. Callinicos, *The Mario Lanza Story*.
11. Specter, *The Pittsburgh Press*, March 1951.
12. Ward, *The Pittsburgh Press*, 7 March 1951.
13. Callinicos, *The Mario Lanza Story*.
14. Callinicos, interview for New Zealand radio, New York 1982. Courtesy British Mario Lanza Society.

Chapter 5
1. Sam Weiler, *Mario Lanza – An American Caruso*, 1983.
2. *Time* magazine, 6 August 1951.
3. Callinicos, radio interview, Columbus, Ohio, June 1974. Courtesy British Mario Lanza Society.

Chapter 6
1. Edmund Purdom, *The Mario Lanza Story*, BBC radio, March 1974.
2. Callinicos, *The Mario Lanza Story*.
3. Callinicos, radio interview, Columbus, Ohio, June 1974. Courtesy British Mario Lanza Society.
4. Callinicos, *The Mario Lanza Story*.
5. Terry Robinson, in conversation with the author.

Chapter 7
1. Licia Albenese, notes from *Mario Lanza in Opera*, RCA Records, 1969.
2. *Time* magazine, 9 April 1956.
3. *Newsweek* magazine, 9 April 1956.
4. *Variety*, April 1956.
5. Callinicos, *The Mario Lanza Story*.

Chapter 8
1. Cyril Ornadel, *The Mario Lanza Story*, BBC radio, March 1974.
2. Sheffield News Review, 5 January 1958.
3. James A. Drake, *Richard Tucker*, (E. P. Dutton Inc., New York, 1984).
4. Callinicos, *The Mario Lanza Story*.
5. John Coast, letter to Mario Lanza, 29 January 1958. Courtesy John Coast Management, London.
6. *Hanoverische Algemein* newspaper, 12 April 1958.
7. Callinicos, *The Mario Lanza Story*.
8. Dr Kurt Klukist, *Lubecher Nachrichten*, Kiel, 14 April 1958.
9. Callinicos, *The Mario Lanza Story*.

Chapter 9
1. Lucie Miller, *Quick* magazine, 1960.
2. Callinicos, interview. Courtesy British Mario Lanza Society.
3. Hermann Hausner, *Tragodie einer Stimme*, (Documenten-Verlag Books, Munich, 1962).
4. Zsa Zsa Gabor, *Mario Lanza – An American Caruso*, 1983.
5. *New York Daily News*, 15 August 1959.
6. *New York Times*, 5 August 1959.
7. *New York Herald Tribune*, 5 August 1959.
8. Richard Mohr. Courtesy Mario Lanza Museum, Philadelphia.
9. Francis Robinson, notes from *Mario Lanza Sings Caruso Favourites*, RCA Records, 1960.

10. Callinicos, *The Mario Lanza Story.*
11. Ibid.
12. Callinicos, radio interview, Columbus, Ohio, June 1974. Courtesy British Mario Lanza Society.
13. Peter Lind Hayes, radio interview, Rome, 30 September 1959.

Chapter 10
1. Callinicos, interview for New Zealand radio, New York 1982. Courtesy British Mario Lanza Society.
2. Ibid.
3. Callinicos, radio interview, Columbus, Ohio, June 1974. Courtesy British Mario Lanza Society.

Contact Addresses

The Mario Lanza Institute, and the Mario Lanza Museum
c/o Settlement Music School
416 Queen Street
Philadelphia
Pennsylvania 19147
USA

The Mario Lanza Educational Foundation
7 Lionfields Avenue
Allesley Village
Coventry CV5 9GN
England

The British Mario Lanza Society (William Earl, chairman)
20 Feversham Close
Shoreham-by-Sea
Sussex BN4 5HD
England

The Mario Lanza Fan Club (Gigi Viciani, president)
Via Italia 61,7
27010 S. Genesio
Italy

Index

173